I0477195

CREATIVE COLLECTIVES

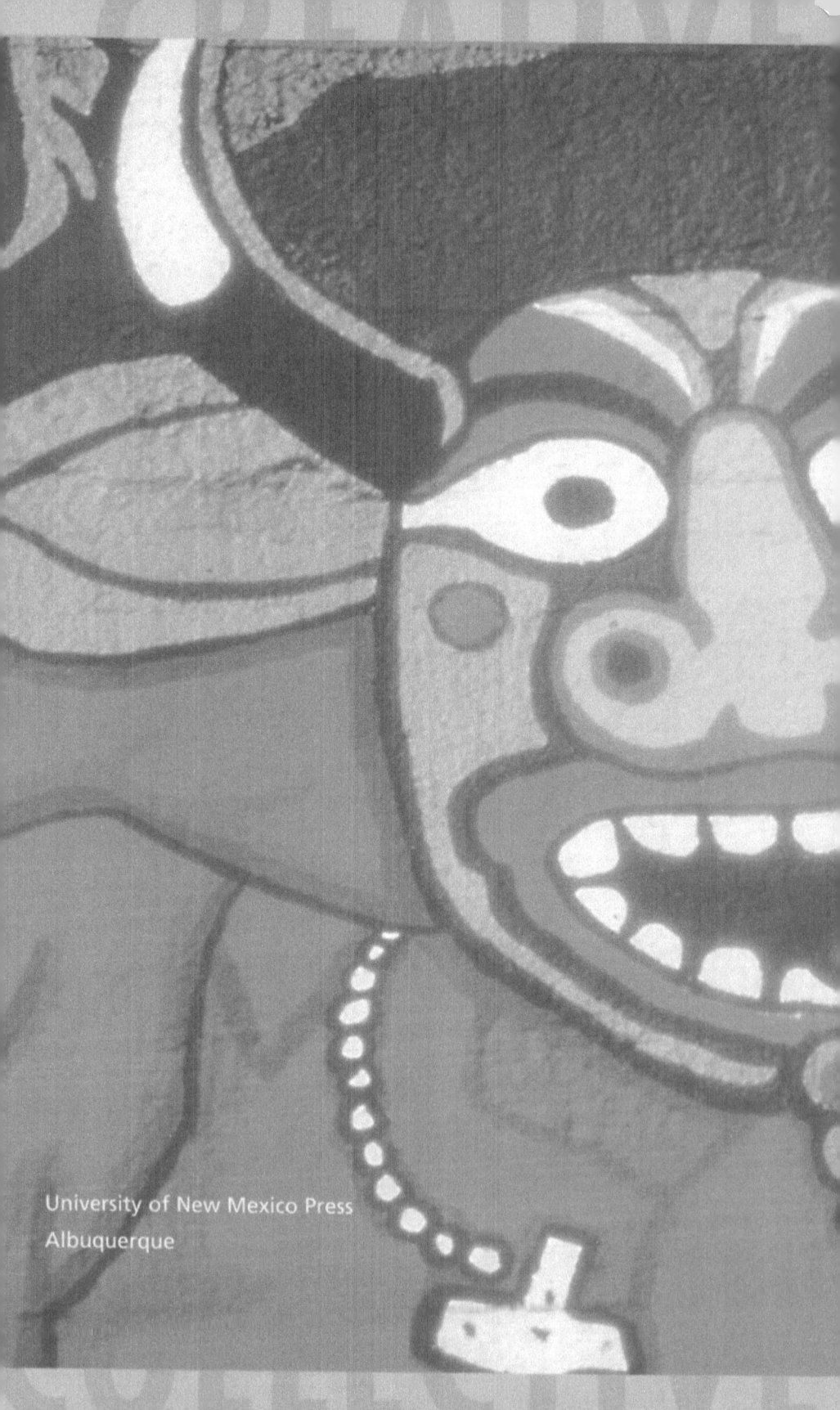

University of New Mexico Press

Albuquerque

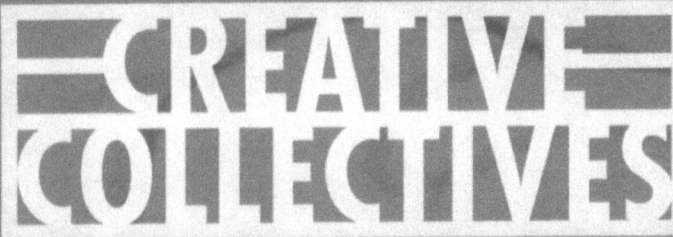

CREATIVE COLLECTIVES

Chicana Painters
Working in Community

María Ochoa

Foreword by Amalia Mesa-Bains

© 2003 by the University of New Mexico Press
All rights reserved. First Edition

Library of Congress Cataloging-in-Publication Data
Ochoa, María, 1950–
Creative collectives : Chicana artists working
in community / María Ochoa.— 1st ed.

p. cm.
Includes bibliographical references and index.
ISBN 0-8263-2110-0 (cloth : alk. paper)
1. Mexican-American art—California, Northern.
2. Women artists—California, Northern. 3. Artists—
California, Northern—Political activity. 4. Feminism and art—
California, Northern. 5. Group work in art—California,
Northern. 6. Ethnicity in art—California, Northern. I. Title.
N6538.M4 O34 2003
704'.042'060794—dc22   2003017864

Cover illustration: Mujeres Muralistas, *Latinoamericana* detail, acryliic on masonry, 20' x 76'. Reproduced with permission of the artists. Photographed by Timothy W. Drescher. Body text set in Frutiger Light and Roman 9.5/13 Display type set in Frutiger Roman and Bold Design and composition: Robyn Mundy

For my mother, **Christine Valtierra Ochoa,**
who taught me to read and dream

For my father, **Anthony William Ochoa** (1922–1988),
who taught me to write and persevere

Contents

List of Plates | viii

Foreword | xi
Amalia Mesa-Bains

Acknowledgments | xiii

Prologue | xv
Never Underestimate the Tenacity
of a Mexican Woman

Introduction | 1
Mujeres y Co-Madres: Creativity
and Collectivity

Chapter 1 | 15
Movements: Departures,
Delays, Arrivals

Chapter 2 | 33
Mujeres Muralistas: "We Offer
You Colors We Make"

Chapter 3 | 59
Co-Madres Artistas: "We Belong
to the Community"

Chapter 4 | 87
Coatlicue's Cartography: Mapping
Hybridity and Creative Collectivity

Plates | 93
The Artistry of Mujeres Muralistas
and Co-Madres Artistas

Bibliography | 125

Index | 135

List of Plates

1. Untitled Balmy Alley mural by Irene Pérez | 94

2. Untitled Balmy Alley mural by Graciela Carrillo and Patricia Rodríguez | 95

3. *Latinoamerica* by Mujeres Muralistas | 96

4. *Latinoamerica* detail | 97

5. *Latinoamerica* detail | 98–9

6. *Latinoamerica* detail | 100–01

7. *Para el Mercado* by Mujeres Muralistas | 102

8. *Para el Mercado* detail | 103

9. *Para el Mercado* detail | 104–5

10. *Para el Mercado* detail | 106–7

11. *Rhomboidal Parallelogram* by Mujeres Muralistas | 108

12. *Rhomboidal Parallelogram* framing for mural | 109

13. *Rhomboidal Parallelogram* detail, Ester Hernández painting her panel | 110

14. *Rhomboidal Parallelogram* detail, Ester Hernández's completed panel | 111

15. *Fantasy World for Children* by Mujeres Muralistas | 112

16. *Fantasy World for Children* detail | 113

17. *La India de la Tierra* by Carmel Castillo | 114

18. *La Curandera* by Carmel Castillo | 115

19. *Warriors of the New Day* by Irma Lerma Barbosa | 116

20. *Chiapas Madonna* by Irma Lerma Barbosa | 117

21. *Self-Portrait in Paradise* by Laura Llano | 118

22. *The Gift* by Laura Llano | 119

23. *Joseph* by Helen Villa | 120

24. *Rene, Esteban, and Nathan* by Helen Villa | 121

25. *The Curtain Rises on Mole* by Mareia de Socorro | 122

26. *The Deer Dances* by Mareia de Socorro | 123

Foreword

In the years since El Movimiento, Chicano/a artists have tried to sustain the values, practices and visual dispositions that made the first period of arts activism so profound. Through the lens provided by María Ochoa's *Creative Collectives: Chicana Painters Working in Community,* we see the connection and the persistence of seminal values and practices in the historic cooperative work of Mujeres Muralistas and in the contemporary collectivity of Co-Madres Artistas. Her analysis of the inner workings of these two groups gives new insight on the strategies and sacrifices that link these artistic collaboratives.

Through oral history interviews and artistic analysis Ochoa brings to life these models of cooperative artistic production. It is the very collective nature of Chicano/a art that sets it apart as a public enterprise devoted to cultural reclamation. Unlike the fine arts model, inspiration is sought in the affirmation of cultural values and untold histories. Ochoa examines the past and binds it to the present through her insightful artistic dialectic encompassing both the personal and the political within two women's collectives from Northern California spanning almost two decades.

This particular inscription of Chicano/a art history bears witness to the struggle of Chicana artists and activists from the founding generation and their present day counterparts. These narratives provide us an artistic genealogy that brings a fuller understanding of the relationship between radical politics, service to community and the visual arts. This book is a thoughtful application of a cultural citizenship that reflects the works of artists whose claims of social, human, and cultural rights help to define their social identities and binding solidarities.

Ochoa foregrounds the artist's voices so that we might reflect on the struggles of space and cultural rights that shaped their communal identity. The first person voices that emerge from the oral history interviews contained in this book are rich in the detail of the artists' daily lives. Through the work of the Mujeres Muralistas and Co-Madres Artistas we acquire an understanding of artistic responsibility and problem solving that brings insight to issues of social justice and visual language. The intimacy and ideology of the artists' lives demonstrates the transformative power of art that is greater than a regional analysis that its focus might imply at first glance.

Creative Collectives is critical to understanding the inextricable relationship between Chicana artistic expression and Chicana feminism. This book's publication and circulation ensures a legacy for future generations, provides a lasting bridge between the past and the future, and takes its place among those invaluable texts that have drawn together Chicano/a art, our lives and our commitments. The individual and collective stories that María Ochoa highlights are compelling and inspiring. Most of all they remind us of the purpose of art and its deep connection to compassion and justice.

Amalia Mesa-Bains, Ph.D.
Director
Visual and Public Art
California State University Monterey Bay

Acknowledgments

How many deserve thanks and recognition for their support in the making of this project? How many stars light the night sky? My family comes first, because without them I would not be. My husband, Michael Sweeney, who is patient, generous, thoughtful, and loving. Mr. B and Rosie teach me to awaken each morning with great optimism for what the day might hold. *Muchas gracias* to my parents, Anthony W. and Christine V. Ochoa, for their encouragement, especially in the arts, and to my sisters, CiCi and Sue, and my brother, Joe, for always showing an interest. One could not ask for a more brilliant and generous group of scholars, Angela Y. Davis, Angie Chabram-Dernersesian, Barbara Epstein, María Eugenia Matute-Bianchi, and Patricia Zavella, who gave of their wise counsel in order for this project to take form. Angela and Pat unstintingly give me encouragement and support and deserve special mention. Early mentors, Vicki Ruíz, Julia Curry-Rodríguez, Wendy Norins, Diane Kerrick, and Barbara Waterman, gave me courage. Friends for life, Barbara Ige, Liz Martín-García, Margaret Rose Daniel, Beatríz López-Flóres, Annie Valva, Teresia Teaiwa, and Lynet Uttal, provided me with love, wisdom, and good humor at various stages of the work. My sextants and compasses at the University of California, Santa Cruz, were Sheila Peuse and Vege Clerisse, as well as the unnamed members of the word processing staff who ably transcribed the oral histories. I offer up thanks to my spirit guides: Bob Marley, La Virgen de Guadalupe, Oceotli, and Sekhmet.

Work such as this is only possible with the financial support of external sources. I want to express my appreciation to the Ford Foundation for a Dissertation Fellowship and a Postdoctoral Fellowship and to the National Women's Studies Association for awarding this project the Pergamon-NWSA First Place Graduate Dissertation/Thesis Scholarship. Seed money was critical in the early stages of the research, and I was fortunate to receive support from several UC Santa Cruz sources: the Center for Cultural Studies, the Chicano/Latino Research Center, and Feminist Studies Focused Research Activities. In addition, I was twice selected as an Oakes College Graduate Associate and twice as a recipient of a Humanities Graduate Studies Fellowship. At some point one must leave home to understand and appreciate its import. A residency with the Humanities Research Institute at the University of California, Irvine, and affiliation with the Stanford Chicana/o Fellows Program contributed a perspective on time and place. University of New Mexico Press staff members, present and past, have been supportive, innovative, and patient: David Holtby, Evelyn Schlatter, Robyn Mundy, Andrea Otañez, and Barbara Guth. Sheila Berg provided crisp clarity with her editor's pencil. Special thanks to Timothy W. Drescher for permission to reproduce his transparencies. Eternal thanks to the artists Ester Hernández, Consuelo Méndez, Irene Pérez, Patricia Rodríguez, Irma Lerma Barbosa, Carmel Castillo, Laura Llano, Mareia de Socorro, and Helen Villa for their permission to reproduce images of their splendid art. The generous and loving spirit of the Mujeres Muralistas and Co-Madres Artistas gives this book its core strength. Each of these women is remarkable for her commitment to social justice and for her work as an artist. ¡Adelante, Mujeres!

Prologue

Never Underestimate the Tenacity of a Mexican Woman

A growing body of scholarship having to do with Chicana artists and their contributions to the visual arts is emerging.[1] Yet its quantity is meager in comparison to the centuries-long cultural contributions made by Mexican women and their contemporary U.S. sisters, Chicanas.[2] This historical lacuna is significant because its existence masks the cultural context and dislocates the historical circumstances of these artistic expressions.[3] This book seeks to remedy, in some measure, the lack of information available to interested artists, scholars, collectors, and community supporters of Chicana/o art. I hope, too, that this text occasions further study of the cultural production and social contributions of Chicana artists. When I reflect on the persistent erasure of the aesthetic contributions by women of Mexican descent, four historical moments stand out as metaphorical and material markers of these absences. I present them here by way of introducing the discussions in this book.

Standing under the hot glare of blazing spotlights, the fiercely majestic basalt statue of the Great Coatlicue looms over the humans crowding around the base, craning and craving to know the mysteries of life and death that the idol embodies. Coatlicue, created in the Aztec year Ce Tochtili, One Rabbit, serves as a tribute to the duality of being: life and death, darkness and light, beginning and end, corporeality and spirituality.[4] It is suggested that the figure was buried in order to protect it from being destroyed by the Spaniards during the early Conquest. It was unearthed in the late sixteenth century and was placed among the Greco-Roman statues already on display at the Royal and Pontifical University of Mexico. Coatlicue's power as an indigenous deity threatened the Roman Catholic orthodoxy, and her imagery offended as well the existing notions of aesthetics.[5] So great was her spiritual influence and so offensive was her visage that the statue was reburied. Coatlicue was exhumed and entombed on several occasions and not permanently disinterred until Mexico became independent of Spanish rule.[6] Today, the power of her aesthetic is internationally acknowledged.

An exhibition, *First Front: Vanguard of the Chicano Movement in Northern California,* was held at La Galería de la Raza in San Francisco during the summer of 1994. It was described as "[a]n exhibition of paintings, graphics, and archival material honoring Chicano artists who launched a tidal wave of artistic expression and the cultural renaissance of the late 1960s–early 1970s."[7] The exhibition was formulated within the cultural nationalist practices that emerged from El Movimiento. As a result of its androcentric approach, not a single Chicana artist was invited to exhibit.[8]

A historical account of the U.S. mural tradition is found in the book *Toward a People's Art: The Contemporary Mural Movement.* Originally published in 1977, it was out of print when this research began in 1990 but reissued in 1998. The artwork on the cover of the second edition includes a detail of *Para el Mercado* painted by Mujeres Muralistas. However, the collective does not receive attribution for their work: the publisher erroneously credits the image to a male muralist.[9]

An exhibition, *Art/Women/California, 1950–2000: Parallels and Intersections,* was held at the San José Museum of Art in 2002. Irene Pérez, Patricia Rodríguez, and Ester Hernández were among the ninety women artists invited to exhibit. Their works of art, along with those of Yolanda López and the Native American artist Jean LaMarr, were placed together in a small basement room next to the museum's bathrooms. Theirs was the only art displayed in this underworld compartment of the museum where the identifying wall label read "Artists and Activism." The remaining eighty-five artists had their works installed on the expansive first- and second-floor galleries. None of these works was placed outside a toilet.[10]

Just as Coatlicue moved from the temple to the museum, the artistic expressions of Chicanas continue to journey from the private sphere to public space.[11] Similar to the Spaniards' disrespect for Coatlicue's significance as a cultural treasure, Chicana artistry is sometimes ignored by the Chicano art community, and largely disregarded (except for the appropriation of certain signifiers) by the mainstream art world. Yet the artists continue to provide valuable contributions to the corpus of Chicana/o art.

Never underestimate the tenacity of a Mexican woman.

Notes

1. Significant contributors include Holly Barnet-Sanchez, Eva Cockcroft, Shifra Goldman, and Amalia Mesa-Bains.
2. Shifra Goldman and Tomás Ybarra-Frausto, comps., *Arte Chicano: A Comprehensive Annotated Bibliography of Chicano Art, 1965–1981* (Berkeley: Chicano Studies Library Publications Unit, University of California, 1985), 32.
3. Amalia Mesa-Bains, "A Study of the Influence of Culture on the Development of Identity among a Group of Chicana Artists" (Ph.D. diss., Wright Institute, 1983), 1.
4. Justino Fernández, *A Guide to Mexican Art, from Its Beginnings to the Present,* trans. Joshua C. Taylor (Chicago: University of Chicago Press, 1969), 42.
5. Octavio Paz, "The Art of Mexico: Material and Meaning," in *Essays on Mexican Art,* trans. Helen Lane (New York: Harcourt Brace & Co., 1993), 31.
6. Ibid.
7. "First Front: Vanguard of the Chicano Movement in Northern California," exhibition announcement card, La Galería de la Raza, San Francisco, August 1994.
8. This gross omission is all the more inexplicable when one considers the many Chicana/Latina visual artists of the Oakland–San Francisco Bay Area who have made significant contributions over the years: Juana Alicia, Graciela Carrillo, Eva García, Lorraine García, Ester Hernández, Carmen Lomas Garza, Yolanda López, Consuelo Méndez, Amalia Mesa-Bains, Xochitl Nevel Guerrero, Irene Pérez, Celia Rodríguez, Patricia Rodríguez, and Linda Lucero, among others.
9. Eva Cockcroft, John Pitman Weber, and James Cockcroft, *Toward a People's Art: The Contemporary Mural Movement,* 2d ed. (Albuquerque: University of New Mexico Press, 1998).
10. John Yau writes of similar treatment of Wifredo Lam's work in "Please Wait by the Cloakroom," in *Out There: Marginalization and Contemporary Cultures,* ed. Russell Ferguson, Martha Gever, and Trinh T. Minh-ha (New York: New Museum of Contemporary Art, 1990).
11. Paz's previously cited essay inspired this metaphor.

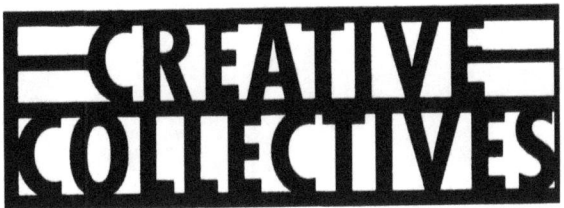

Mujeres y Co-Madres

Creativity and Collectivity

This book looks at the ways in which two groups of northern California Chicana/Latina artists, Mujeres Muralistas and Co-Madres Artistas, developed as creative collectives within different periods of the Chicana/o Art Movement. The core discussion emerges from highlighting the individual processes of the subject artists, as well as from examining the constitutive elements of their art, including the effect of collectively produced artwork. The root argument of this book is that the artistic works of these women were first seeded within the quotidian elements of Chicana/o life and flowered in the presence of Chicana feminist thought and practice. This book further argues that it was through the cultural particularity of their artistic expression that these Chicanas enunciated themselves as collectives and endowed themselves with social agency. By interpolating personal histories within representational analyses, this book demonstrates how the individual members developed artistic styles that resulted in representations that both affirmed the artists' identities within the Chicana/o community and served as expressions of resistance to the hegemony of mainstream culture. This study also illustrates how the artwork serves as a means for communicating the artists' varied positionalities within the differentiated activities of their daily lives.

The stories of Mujeres Muralistas and Co-Madres Artistas are foregrounded because each group has particular significance in the evolution of the Chicana/o Art Movement. Members of both groups were active in the early years of the movement and are participants even today.

Their personal histories are placed against the backdrop of the Chicana/o Art Movement and U.S. Third World feminism. As a result of this multi-leveled approach, the collective narratives provide a measure of understaning of how groups whose memberships consist primarily of Chicana artists successfully combine the work of artist and activist in a collaborative environment. This success is no small accomplishment as each of the artists brings a particular consciousness, a unique artistic style and ability, and specific social characteristics, such as class background, sexual orientation, cultural, and ethnic heritage, to the collective. Because these complex social circumstances contribute to the successes and challenges of each collective, they also serve as subjects for discussion.

Organized during the early 1970s, Mujeres Muralistas was a mural painting collective consisting of Chicana and Latina artists who lived and worked in the Oakland–San Francisco Bay Area. This group of college-educated, formally trained artists, between the ages of nineteen and twenty-five, converged in San Francisco from different home places in California, as well as from Texas and South America. The collective consisted of four core artists, three of whom identify themselves as Chicanas and one as Latina. In addition, four assistants, three Chicanas and one white woman, came in and out of the group's projects. Although one member comes from a middle-class family, the majority of the artists involved have working-class backgrounds, including farmworker families. Three of the four artists interviewed for this book attended the San Francisco Art Institute; the fourth attended the University of California, Berkeley. Some of the artists are mothers. Some members were involved in heterosexual relationships at the onset of the group, and two of the artists identify themselves as lesbians.

During the time that the collective created their murals, self-definition as an artist was central for those who were core artists, and there was a more emergent process for the assistants. All of the artists were involved in the thriving arts community that was developing in Oakland–San Francisco Bay Area. La Galería de la Raza was one of the cultural centers that emerged during this period, and the artists were to varying degrees engaged in its early history. As of this writing, all of the Mujeres Muralistas who participated in this study are practicing artists. One lives in South America and exhibits internationally. Three live in the Bay Area, where two work as art teachers; all three participate in exhibitions globally. They all work in various media, including installation, lithography, decorative arts, electronic, and mural painting.

Six women founded Co-Madres Artistas in 1992. Their ages at the time ranged from forty-four to sixty-five. In addition to the six artist members, the collective included an administrator whose work enabled the artists to focus on the creative elements of their work. Most of the members are college educated and formally trained as artists and were born and raised in the Sacramento Valley. Those who are not native to the area have lived in the valley for more than thirty years. The Chicana/o community of Sacramento contributes to a vibrant cultural legacy that is reflected throughout the history of the Chicana/o Art Movement. Groups such as the Royal Chicano Air Force (RCAF), institutions such as La Raza Galería Posada, and businesses such as Café Luna have long histories in Sacramento stemming from the early years of the movement. Co-Madres Artistas members played important roles in the founding and ongoing work necessary to keep these institutions alive for so many years.

Acquisition of a college education played an important role in the prefigurative years of Co-Madres Artistas members. The State College, now known as Sacramento State University, was where many of the women acquired their undergraduate degrees during the 1970s. In addition to their domestic responsibilities, all of the members labor outside of the home. The majority of the members work in administrative positions for various state agencies in arenas unrelated to the arts. All members have at least one child and identify as heterosexual. At some point, all of the members were married, although not all were married or in primary relationships at the time of the interviews.

Members of the two groups share similarities with respect to college education, involvement in community-based cultural organizations, and engagement in the Chicana/o Art Movement. That each of the artists in Mujeres Muralistas and Co-Madres Artistas received her foundational training in institutions of higher learning is remarkable. Ana Nieto Gómez's research, published in 1974, when the women of Mujeres Muralistas and Co-Madres Artistas were in college, amplifies the rarity of this experience. Gómez notes that during this period, 70 percent of Chicanas dropped out of high school by the tenth grade.[1] Receiving a college education is uncommon for the majority of Chicanas even now.[2] In the absence of institutions that respected Chicana/o cultural work, artists founded their own organizations as venues for exhibition, performance, and convocation. Mujeres Muralistas members were important in the development of La Galería de la Raza, as were the Co-Madres Artistas to the ongoing work of La Raza Galería Posada. Their social justice involvement embraced, then as now, other facets of the Chicana/o Movement, including the struggles of the United Farm Worker's Union. Before their respective formation as collectives, Mujeres Muralistas members provided art classes for children and painted murals in community centers; Co-Madres Artistas members volunteered at breakfast and tutoring programs for children.

Movidas/Methodologies

In this book, I use a qualitative social research approach and representational analysis. The oral history methodology that is elemental to this narration relies on Chicana/Latina feminist ethnographic methods such as those employed by Patricia Zavella, Ruth Behar, and Rina Benmayor. These scholars were influential in the formulation of the methodology of this project because they are each committed to the study of the quotidian in the development of contemporary Latinas' roles, and they place particular emphasis on dialogic approaches in their oral history work. The representational analysis is grounded in Chicana/o art history and critique. Works by Amalia Mesa-Bains, Timothy W. Drescher, Tomás Ybarra-Frausto, Shifra Goldman, and Jacinto Quirarte influenced this portion of the research. While each historian has a unique set of interests and approaches to the study of the Chicana/o Art Movement, what they share is a narrative style notable for its intertextual weaving of social, art, and individual histories of artists with representational analyses. Angie Chabram-Dernersesian describes the possibilities born of this multidisciplinary approach:

> The critical re-examination of the writing of cultures through oral histories and ethnographies can provide a basis for grasping a condition which does not appear in text books and which is contained by traditional forms of discourse that impose an analogical structure on their subject matter.[3]

This book is concerned specifically with the artistic and social approaches employed by two groups of Chicanas as they developed their unique forms of artistic and cultural representation that, in turn, emerged from their individual and group identities. Avtar Brah describes how such methodologies of identity construction emerge from the ideological parameters that define collective processes: "Identities are relational and contextual [and one must] look for the relations that exist among these positions in specific contexts, and the ways these positions are themselves produced by context."[4] In crafting this study so as to emphasize the idelogical face of Mexican American identity, three categories are denoted: Chicana/o, Chicana, and Chicano. I borrow from Yolanda Broyles-González, who deploys the category "Chicana/o" in order to overtly reference Chicanas and foreground gender; Chicano is left unchanged when it refers to something male or male centered.[5]

To emphasize the cultural specificity of a discussion, a Spanish-language word, such as *mujer,* is used. Women of European descent are referenced similarly by using the term "Anglo women." The categories "U.S. women of color" and "U.S. Third World women" are also invoked throughout this project. Both references borrow from Chandra Talpade Mohanty, who evokes them to describe women living in the United States who are racially descended from *and* culturally engaged in the practices of any of the following peoples: African, Asian, Caribbean, Latin, Pacific Islander, and Middle Eastern, including those of Sephardic Jewish descent, as well as U.S. indigenous populations.[6]

Mujeres Muralistas and Co-Madres Artistas are referred to as creative collectives. By naming them as such, it is intended that the artists be understood as cultural workers whose practices reckon the inclusion of community interaction as they develop their paintings.[7] Intrinsic to their work as artists is the conscious spirit of collaborative endeavor. Mujeres Muralistas operated and Co-Madres Artistas operate as collective entities whose artistic energies reside within the production of community-oriented and public art forms and whose imagery insists on political and ethnic themes.[8]

Because socially conscious artists do not view their work as separate from movement politics, it is crucial to emphasize the indivisibility of Chicana/o artistic production from Chicana/o activism. The creation and circulation of artistic expression is critical to understanding the creative articulation of the liberation movement. The artwork produced by the artists in this history is embedded in the struggle for social justice, just as the word "art" is embedded in the Chicana/o Art Movement. As I wrote this book, it became important to me to disrupt a casual reading of the words Chicana/o Art Movement. I wanted to highlight the pivotal role of Chicana/o artists in the fight for self-determination, just as the contributions of Chicana/o artists are intended, in part, to disrupt the visual continuity of mainstream aesthetics. Although I struggled to find a way to mark the word "art" in the descriptive phrase Chicana/o Art Movement, all of the formats I considered, such as underscoring or italicizing, seemed lacking. Using parentheses seemed counter to the intent, as the artists and the artwork are clearly not parenthetical to the movement. I decided to let the phrase stand without special formatting. I hope that readers will inflect the word "art" when it appears in the phrase "Chicana/o Art Movement."[9]

Reflejo en el Espejo: Reflections of the Process and of Myself

Methodological choices are complex, often made in situ, mostly less rational than the textbook versions, and moreover, rather boring to recount, except from the point of view of the researcher herself, for whom the whole experience has something of the feel of an heroic epic.[10]

The above quotation is intended as a caveat: the discussion here focuses on the practices that shaped my research, including the way in which I questioned my role in the development of the book. By sharing this information, I hope to provide an understanding of the optic used to focus this work and to furnish some insight regarding my personal interrogation of "the sanctioned ignorance of my own ethnographic authority."[11]

The central approach that guided the qualitative social research portion of this study is that of the oral history collection process, as described by Sherna Berger Gluck and Daphne Patai: "Oral history refers to the whole enterprise: recording, transcribing, editing, and making public the resulting product—usually but not necessarily a written text."[12] Patricia Zavella, Rina Benmayor, Ruth Behar, Ruth Frankenberg, and Renato Rosaldo influence this project, and inflections of their work are perceptible to varying degrees in my approach. Zavella, who maps the contours of social relations among working women in culturally specific locations, was an early influence.[13] While I was developing a lens through which I sharpened my own vision, I relied on what she and others call "practice anthropology." Zavella, working with Louise Lamphere, Felipe Gonzales, and Peter B. Evans, says of this methodology:

Our approach is that of "practice anthropology," viewing women's behavior at work and at home as "praxis": the outcome of experience, of day-to-day trial and error in pushing against and coping with the requirements of a particular job, negotiating with a husband over housework, or dealing with the demands of a child. We see women as active agents who develop strategies for managing their everyday lives.[14]

By borrowing from this methodology, I am able to extrapolate the various ways in which the artists of Mujeres Muralistas and Co-Madres Artistas draw intellectual, creative, and emotional strength from the quotidian experiences of their lives. My research approach has also benefited from Rina Benmayor's ongoing ethnographic studies of Puerto Rican women. Her collaborative scholarship regarding the dynamic of Latina/o "cultural citizenship" is an important contribution to understanding Latina/o formulations of community.[15] In the context of this project it is her demarcation of cultural citizenship as a series of affirming acts that arise out of the quotidian that is most resonant with my interests. Writing in concert with William V. Flóres, Benmayor elaborates:

> In our opinion, what makes cultural citizenship so exciting is that it offers us an alternative perspective to better comprehend the cultural processes that result in community building and in political claims raised by marginalized group. . . . Cultural citizenship can be thought of as a broad range of activities of everyday life through which Latinos and other groups claim space in society and eventually claim rights. Although it involves difference, it is not as if Latinos seek out such difference. Rather, the motivation is simply to create space where the people feel "safe" and "at home," where they feel a sense of belonging and membership.[16]

My work is further informed by Benmayor's understanding and interpretation of the vernacular and its centrality in the development of collective agency. Benmayor, again, working with others, describes the construct: "We argue for the need to understand vernacular expressions of culture and collective agency in historical and structural context. That is, cultural claims for equality need to be appreciated from the perspective of people themselves as social agents."[17] This formulation was especially important in coming to understand the collaborative relationships that developed for each of the groups. Both Mujeres Muralistas and Co-Madres Artistas owed their artistic strength to their collectivity; their claim to territory within the landscape of the Chicana/o Art Movement was enabled by their potency as a group. To paraphrase one of the members of Co-Madres Artistas: "Individually we are not so significant, but as a group we are giants."[18]

In researching the individual and collective histories of Mujeres Muralistas and Co-Madres Artistas, I interviewed fifteen women and men between 1992 and 1994; one interview occurred in 1999. All of the subjects were central contributors to the formation of the groups under study here. The majority of the artists live in northern California. These interviews were primarily conducted in the living and work spaces of the subjects, although two interviews took place at the participants' work sites, and one was conducted by telephone with an artist living in South America. The general approach used to contact the artists was similar but by no means exactly the same. For example, since Mujeres Muralistas was no longer creating as a group, I contacted individual former members. In an initial telephone conversation, I described the project and my relationship to it and the rationale for selecting Mujeres Muralistas. I encouraged questions, although the artists were savvy enough to know they did not require my encouragement, and found that my personal history and experiences as an artist and activist came under scrutiny most often. Subsequent to this discussion, I mailed a brief description of the study to the artist and followed up with a second telephone call to arrange an interview and to answer any additional questions that may have come to mind.

In the case of Co-Madres Artistas I initially made contact with the group through a telephone number provided in their promotional materials. We arranged for me to attend a regularly scheduled meeting of the group. At this meeting, where all but one member was present, I gave a brief summary of the proposed project and then stopped for questions. The women's queries focused on my personal history, my interest in art, and my intended publication of the material generated by their interviews. After a two-hour discussion I left with a unanimous affirmative response from the group. Following this meeting, I mailed the group a copy of a previous research project of mine, so that they might have a more concrete example of my approach. I then followed up with telephone calls to individual members to answer questions and arrange appointments for the interviews.

All participating artists were asked to meet with me for a preliminary interview. Our discussions were one on one and open-ended and covered the following general areas: the formation of the group, when and how the individual became involved with the group, and the group's successes and conflicts. We also discussed the artist's views regarding her artistic development and the effect of the group on her creative style and personal identity. Our interview explored ideas regarding the relationship of art to social activism, especially within the Chicana/o Art Movement. This portion of the dialogue included participants' descriptions of their personal and collective development as well as their contributions as activists. Those artists who met with me in their home studios invariably brought out samples of their work to illustrate historical moments in their evolution as artists or to underscore certain points regarding their representations. This was always a richly illuminating moment; the presence of the artwork energized our discussions and made for a lively dialogue on matters of artistic intent and audience reception.

A consent form was provided to each artist at the time of the interview. Participants were informed that the interviews would be audiotape recorded and that they could receive copies of the audiotape and the transcription. They were able to withdraw from the project at any point prior to the publication of the material. Refusal to answer particular questions was always an option for participants. Most artists chose either to ask that I turn off the tape recorder or to make it clear that the information they were providing was for "my ears only." Thus the participants were able to offer important details, knowing that it would not be shared or made public in any way. The type of information that was told to me under these conditions had to do primarily with interpersonal relationships and conflicts among the artists in the groups.

Most of the time we worked in the traditional manner of interviewer and interviewee. All interviews were taped and transcribed. Each artist was offered a copy of the tape and the transcription and invited to comment. Some elected to share the editorial changes, corrections, and updates in writing, others by telephone, and still others via email. All participants conferred with me after the initial draft. Most of the artists interviewed for this study responded to the manuscript on two occasions. Although I was not inclined to operate through a traditional "objective" approach, it was also clear that I needed to be cautious of the limitations of subjectivity. I tried to remain mindful of Renato Rosaldo's caution on the matter of positioning oneself as a closely engaged, yet self-reflexive researcher:

> If distance has certain arguable advantages, so too does closeness, and both have their deficits. . . . Social analysts should explore their subjects from a number of positions, rather than being locked into any particular one. . . . Cultures and their "positioned subjects" are laced with power, and power in turn is shaped by cultural forms.[19]

Interpolation of the Self

As I consider the many ways in which I implicated and inserted myself into this research and the narrative that exists here, I return to three benchmark moments embedded in my memory of the past. As a youth I accompanied my parents to numerous community meetings. One evening we entered a church hall where people convivially jostled for space and hailed each other between bites of *pan dulce* and sips of hot coffee. At some point before the start of the meeting, my eyes fixed on a banner whose simple imagery and use of color commanded my attention: a solitary black bird juxtaposed against a white circle dropped onto a field of vibrant red. I recall nothing of the words spoken that evening, but I always remember where I was when I first saw the emblem of the United Farm Workers Union. That moment marked the first time in my life that I was conscious of the way in which art could sustain itself in my imagination.

Similarly, the artwork of Mujeres Muralistas grabbed my attention at a moment when I was not expecting to be moved. An overcast morning in 1975 found me walking to a friend's home in San Francisco's Mission District. While en route I happened upon the mural *Latinoamerica*. I was enthralled by its vibrant colors and celebratory spirit. That a group of *mujeres* was responsible for this visual paean of Latina/o culture fueled my admiration.[20]

Fifteen years later, I experienced the terrifying freedom of developing a dissertation project. Still inspired by the paintings of Mujeres Muralistas and aware of the individual artists' prodigious creative endeavors and enduring commitment to community-based art, I began to seek materials regarding these artists. My nascent exploration produced a paltry sum of dated information. As my intellectual desire to know more grew, the vision of this project emerged. Habitually on the prowl for information on any and all Chicana artists, I heard from a friend wanting to slake my appetite for data. She mailed a package and included a note that read, "Got this today and thought of you. Hope it helps."[21] It was a "catalogue of fine art" produced by a collective that called themselves Co-Madres Artistas.

•   •   •

As a Chicana native to California with some college training as a visual artist, I shared a somewhat similar background with many of the mujeres whom I interviewed. My ethnic, sexual, cultural, and class status as a "peer" of the artists complicated my role as an interviewer, as an "outsider." I faced the conundrum that emerges "when the 'ethnographic others' are from the same society, same race or ethnicity, gender, and class backgrounds as the ethnographer."[22] As a woman of color working in the traditions of ethnographic fieldwork, I was uncomfortable with the legacy of cultural observation that this form of research implied. Ruth Behar captures well the unease that I experienced and the circuitous internal path I developed in order to conduct the research:

> With all the discussion of ethnographic writing going on at the moment, so little is said about how each of us comes to pen and the computer and the authority to speak and author texts. . . . [A]uthorship is a privilege to which many of us are not born, but arrive at, often clumsily, often painfully, often through a process of self-betrayal and denial.[23]

In the process of situating myself with the participants, the artists let me know that they appreciated my desire to craft a well-formulated narrative. They were glad to have their stories told, and they were also aware that the interests of my research project were not necessarily theirs. They reminded me that my analysis was a text that eventually would be directed to an academic community. Such frank and caring commentary better enabled me to accept and acknowledge the obvious power dynamic that shaped the research and my relationships with the artists. There was an imbalance in power relations in the sense that I set the agenda for inquiry, edited the material, and analyzed it. The time framework of and settings for the interviews were defined by the work and family schedules of the artists. The majority of the interviews took place in the artists' domestic spaces and, with rare exception, began at the kitchen table. One interview took place while the artist and I sorted out the pebbles from the frijoles in preparation for that evening's dinner. Another interview moved from the family vegetable garden, where I assisted in harvesting lettuce, to the kitchen, where we canned tomatoes. Yet another took place during a woman's lunch hour on the steps of a civic building near her work while pedestrian traffic and automobiles swirled around us. Another occurred in the middle of an art school for developmentally disabled adults, where the ambient noise made careful listening and close engagement a series of challenges. Later, while trying to develop the transcript from the audiotaped interview, the transcriptionist complained that the background noise prevented her from hearing the dialogue. She was also exasperated by the occasional lapses of English into Spanglish. She quit the project.

In addition to the transcriptions of the interviews, other materials relevant to the formulation of this project included photographs and transparencies of original artwork, self-descriptive writing from the artists, periodical reviews of the artists' exhibitions, exhibition announcement cards and catalogues, and personal correspondence, including email messages. In the case of Mujeres Muralistas, only one of the murals selected for discussion still exists. All other art of theirs was remarked on by using photographs and transparencies. The original artwork by the Co-Madres Artistas was made available to me for study. I was also able to reference their work through the use of an exhibition catalogue and transparencies.

Before leaving this discussion, I want to underscore the fact that this book is not intended to offer up the artists of Mujeres Muralistas and Co-Madres Artistas or their artwork as the definitive experiences and characteristics of Chicana/Latina artists or of Chicana/Latina aesthetics. The stories told here reflect but a sliver of time in the rich and complex lives of the women involved in the two collectives. As Frankenberg reminds us: "An interview is not, in any simple sense, the telling of a life so much as it is an incomplete story angled toward [one's] questions and each woman's ever-changing sense of self and of how the world works."[24]

Outline of the Book

Chapter 1 provides a series of reflections intended to provide some understanding of the Chicana/o Art Movement, Chicana feminist thought, and U.S. Third World feminism and their influences on the development of Chicana artists and their creative expressions. Chapters 2 and 3 are focused on the stories of Mujeres Muralistas and Co-Madres Artistas. Each narrative describes the preformative stage of the collective as well as the period in which the group matured in their collaborative production of visual art. The oral histories detail questions of group dynamics and influences that are woven into discussions regarding the representational decisions of the artists. The purpose of the concluding chapter is to summarize, review, and reflect on the social processes and artistic representations of Mujeres Muralistas and Co-Madres Artistas. Color reproductions of the artworks referred to in the body of the oral history chapters are presented in the appendix.

Notes

1. Ana Nieto Gómez, "Chicanas in the Labor Force," *Encuentro Feminil* 1, no. 2 (1974).
2. Deborah J. Wilds, "Students of Color Make Gains in Higher Education," *American Council on Education Office of Minorities in Higher Education 17th Annual Status Report* 49, no. 3 (2000): 2. "Hispanics continued to significantly trail whites in the percentage of adults ages 25 to 29 with a bachelor's degree or higher. Nearly 29 percent of whites in this age group had at least a bachelor's degree in 1997 (up from 24 percent in 1990 and 1980), compared with only 11 percent of Hispanics (up from 8.1 percent and 7.7 percent)."
3. Angie Chabram-Dernersesian, "Chicana/o Studies as Oppositional Ethnography," *Cultural Studies: Special Issue on Chicana/o Cultural Representations* 4, no. 3 (1990).
4. Avtar Brah, "Questions of Difference and International Feminism," in *Out of the Margins: Women's Studies in the Nineties,* ed. Jane Aaron and Sylvia Walby (London: Falmer Press, 1991), 169.
5. Yolanda Broyles-González, *El Teatro Campesino: Theater in the Chicano Movement* (Austin: University of Texas Press, 1994), xviii.
6. Chandra Talpade Mohanty, "Cartographies of Struggle: Third World Women and the Politics of Feminism," in *Third World Women and the Politics of Feminism,* ed. Chandra Talpade Mohanty, Ann Russo, and Lourdes Torres (Bloomington: Indiana University Press, 1991), 4.
7. Eva Cockcroft, John Pitman Weber, and James Cockcroft, *Toward a People's Art: The Contemporary Mural Movement,* 2d ed. (Albuquerque: University of New Mexico Press, 1998), 108.
8. Shifra Goldman and Tomás Ybarra-Frausto, comps., *Arte Chicano: A Comprehensive Annotated Bibliography of Chicano Art, 1965–1981* (Berkeley: Chicano Studies Library Publications Unit, University of California, 1985), 32.
9. *Gracias* to Dr. Barbara K. Ige, a brilliant scholar, excellent teacher, and dear friend whose thoughtfully energetic discussions inform my writing here.
10. Ruth Frankenberg, *White Women, Race Matters: The Social Construction of Whiteness* (Minneapolis: University of Minnesota Press, 1993).
11. Ruth Behar, *Translated Woman: Crossing the Border with Esperanza's Story* (Boston: Beacon Press, 1993), 340.
12. Sherna Berger Gluck and Daphne Patai, eds., *Women's Words: The Feminist Practice of Oral History* (London: Routledge, 1991).
13. See Patricia Zavella, *Women's Work and Chicano Families: Cannery Workers of the Santa Clara Valley* (Ithaca: Cornell University Press, 1987); Louise Lamphere, Patricia Zavella, Felipe Gonzáles, with Peter B. Evans, *Sunbelt Working Mothers: Reconciling Family and Factory* (Ithaca: Cornell University Press, 1993).
14. Lamphere et al., *Sunbelt Working Mothers,* 17.
15. In describing the ways in which northern New Mexican Hispana weavers organized themselves as a cooperative venture, I rely on the concept of cultural citizenship as articulated by Benmayor and others. María Ochoa, "Cooperative Re/Weavings," *Perspectives in Mexican American Studies,* Mexican American Studies and Research Center, University of Arizona 5 (1996).
16. William V. Flóres and Rina Benmayor, eds., *Latino Cultural Citizenship: Claiming Identity, Space, and Rights* (Boston: Beacon Press, 1997), 15.
17. Ibid., 154.

18. Mareia de Socorro, telephone communication, July 7, 2002.

19. Renato Rosaldo, *Culture and Truth: The Remaking of Social Analysis* (Boston: Beacon Press, 1989), 169.

20. Two years later, while working at a multiservice center for women, I secured funding for and coordinated a CETA program for muralists. In tribute to the artists who inspired the formation of the program, it was named Las Mujeres Muralistas de Hayward. Three senior artists were hired to design, paint, and teach mural techniques to thirty students hired through a youth employment program. It was messy, complex, and exhilarating, and for a few years our city was dotted with their art. None of the works exist today, except in photographs and memories.

21. Thanks to Lynn Rogers, then Executive Consultant to the Alameda County Art Commission, for sending me the information that would move this research to another level.

22. Patricia Zavella, "Feminist Insider Dilemmas: Constructing Identity with 'Chicana' Informants," *Frontiers: A Journal of Women's Studies* 13, no. 3 (1992).

23. Behar, *Translated Woman,* 338.

24. Frankenberg, *White Women, Race Matters,* 41.

ONE

Movements

Departures, Delays, Arrivals

In charting the peregrination of Chicana artists as they traveled within the ideological boundaries of several liberation movements, I seek to demonstrate how they and others of their generation were indelibly marked with a spirit of progressive activism and commitment to cultural engagement. The stories of the individual members of the collectives Mujeres Muralistas and Co-Madres Artistas demonstrate the strategies they used to affirm their ideas and practices of organization and self-representation. Their individual approaches resulted from an everyday strategy of resistance as they negotiated life in an Anglo-dominated society. Operating as a collective, each group developed mutually bound actions that permitted them agency in the realm of social change and cultural exchange. By studying these groups as creative collectives, a map emerges that enables a critical exploration of the topography over which these Chicanas traveled to arrive at their expressions of collaborative artistry. This cultural cartography also permits the discovery of the different strategies deployed by Chicana artists as they resisted the hegemonic structures and strictures of incorporation, objectification, and fragmentation.

Each group subverted fixed notions about collective identification and the development of visual representation. Combining the work of artist and activist and carrying out that work in collaboration with others is a complex task. Every relationship, every creation, every decision is shot through with power imbalances and inequities that emanate from the individuals involved and are created by external social conditions. By looking at the methods and artistry of Mujeres Muralistas, we learn about Chicana visual art produced during the early stages of the Chicana/o Art Movement. We also become acquainted with the cooperative artistic processes practiced during this period.[1] Studying the methods and products of Co-Madres Artistas provides insight into the approaches of mature artists and illustrates the assertion that the 1980s were "a period of renewed vitality that resulted in greater recognition for Chicano art and new opportunities for Chicano artists."[2] In the aggregate, these histories demonstrate how two small but highly committed groups of Chicanas developed potent artistic forms of oppositionality that arose out of their everyday lives. We also come to understand how their artwork provided the means for their audiences to contextualize and reflect on the daily realities of their lives.

Both collectives established modes of production that permitted individual creativity in the context of cooperative decision making. Their formulations allowed them to make significant contributions in the development of oppositional culture through their work as artists. The processes and artistry of Mujeres Muralistas and Co-Madres Artistas should be understood as "having generated new meanings and values, new practices, new significations, and experiences."[3] Raymond Williams defines emergent culture as derivative of a series of practices that can be alternative or oppositional. In his view, "[A]lternative cultural practices occur when someone finds a different way to live and wishes to be left alone with it. . . . [O]ppositional cultural practices are identifiable when someone finds a different way to live and wants to change the society in its light."[4]

By developing strategies that ran counter to the prevailing constructs of Chicana femaleness, the women of Mujeres Muralistas and Co-Madres Artistas forged a hybrid approach to their artistry. This cultural work was directly linked to their variegated identities as Chicanas operating at the nexus of the Chicano Movement and U.S. Third World feminism. Many Chicanas located themselves as agents of social change within the Chicana/o Movement and as allies with feminists, especially women of color. To understand how the artists operated within these dual poles of activism, it is important to identify benchmark moments in the evolution of each of the movements. We must examine the ways in which both sources of activism permitted Chicanas' engagement and, in some instances, limited engagement in these ideological discourses and political praxes.

The Movement of Chicanas

During the 1960s, liberation movements initiated mass mobilizations calling for social justice. Several iterations of Chicano activism, including farmworker, civil rights, student, antiwar, and land grant issues, were unified under the banner of the Chicano Movement. By offering these discrete struggles as an aggregated whole, the ideological space for people of Mexican descent to articulate and assert a collective identity emerged. However, the unproblematized presentation of a unified movement resulted in a range of tensions, not the least of which was "a political debate between Chicanas and Chicanos based on the internal gender contradictions."[5] A paradoxical quality, shared by the various movements, emerged from the presumed egalitarian orientation of the mobilizations for social justice and the organizational disregard for matters pertaining to women.[6]

The gendered contradictions emerged within the Chicano Movement from its foundational logic wherein a narrowly defined articulation of *mestizaje* culture included the "glorification and romanticization of the Chicano family and the traditional role of women within the family."[7] Identification as a Chicano was intended to foster an oppositional consciousness through emphasis on cultural pride as a source of ideological unity. However, by constructing the movement through the traditional hierarchical family structure, men were allocated a central space from which to operate and women were relegated to a subordinated position. The presentation of mestiza/o identity contained the seeds for a blossoming egalitarianism within the movement, but the particular form of identity that emerged as the articulated essence of mestizaje ignored a wide range of historical and social constructs through which to define this form of cultural identity.

The dominant formulation of mestiza/o consciousness was constructed through the historical encounter between the Spanish imperialist forces and the indigenous cultures of the Americas. Chicano activists sought to subvert the colonial history of the Spanish in the Americas by diminishing the European portion of the equation and valorizing the indigenous aspect of mestizaje.[8] Scant attention was paid to the fact that the mestiza/o traditions for some Chicanas/os emerged as the historical result of the Middle Passage that brought Africans to the Americas as slaves. Others claimed their mestiza/o identity as the progeny of Sephardic Jews who fled from Mediterranean countries in the thirteenth and fourteenth centuries and arrived in the Americas as refugees. While the landscape of mestizaje was intended to provide an ideological space in which to articulate a politics of liberation, its impermeability instead created and sustained a Chicano cultural nationalism that was persistently separatist in its enunciation and androcentric in its internal logic. Although Chicanas urged attention to the misogynist tendencies embedded in the emergent liberation movement, their arguments largely went unheeded. Occasional gestures were made toward a construct of a Chicana/o liberation movement that included mujeres as compatriots. But for the most part agency, especially within the leadership of El Movimiento, was limited to "carnales y chingónes."[9]

One leader who elected not to operate solely within the space of cultural nationalism was César E. Chávez. As a labor organizer, Chávez recognized the need to build alliances with workers beyond his base of Chicanos and Mexicans, and he was successful in creating linkages with Filipinas/os, Anglos, and African Americans laboring in the fields.[10] He encouraged and worked with women, most notably Dolores Huerta, in leadership positions in the fledgling union.[11] Although Chávez created successful cross-cultural alliances and expanded the role of women, especially Chicanas, men in the Chicano Movement leadership ignored his positive results.

In this context, the material and representational space allocated to Chicanas permitted a limited range of roles, primarily having to do with domestic matters, in particular with the servicing of Chicanos' needs. Chicanas who questioned these aspects of the movement suffered the consequences of their feminist analyses by being labeled *vendidas* (sellouts) or *agabachadas* (anglicized).[12] Needless to say, these social and political sanctions were intended to discourage Chicanas from articulating feminist critiques.[13] This punitive approach, however, did not silence Chicanas altogether. In her 1969 essay, "¡Despierten Mujeres!" Enriqueta Longeaux Vasquez describes the ways in which Chicanas were relegated to subordinate positions in the fledgling movement. She links her argument to the indigenous past and in the process subverts the androcentric model of the family deployed by Chicanos in the construct of mestizaje:

> When we look at and talk about the Raza woman, we have to really think seriously and realize that we are dealing with a real mixed up side of the social battle. The woman has been stereotyped as a servant to the man and the Raza has come to accept this as a great *tradition*. . . . Well, Compadre after doing some thinking and reading, I'll have to blow up that little bubble dream for us. . . . It looks to me as if this continent had a highly *civilized* way of life. . . . The

Europeans certainly destroyed a good thing ¿Que no? And now we talk of the tradition of the woman and say, "No, we must not change the role of the woman, the woman must remain totally dominated in order to keep this tradition." Let's take another look at this family "tradition" the men say we have. Remember we are Mestizos, a people of Spanish fathers and Indian mothers. Male domination over the woman is a thing of Spain and Europe. Destroying the Indian woman's freedom was necessary in order to conquer and destroy the Indian. . . . When we look at all of this and see our real history and heritage, we come to realize that a strong Raza woman is inevitable.[14]

Other early critical works, such as those by Ana Nieto Gómez and Marta Cotera, resonated with the experiences of numerous Chicanas struggling to overcome the misogynistic tendencies of the movement. Nieto Gómez's 1974 essay, "La Feminista," in the founding issue of *Encuentro Feminil,* the first-ever published Chicana feminist journal, and Cotera's 1976 work, *Diosa y Hembra: The History and Heritage of Chicanas in the United States,* opened new avenues of theoretical and praxis-related expressions available to Chicanas.[15] Nieto Gómez and Cotera brought rigorous scholarship and compelling arguments to their work as they quantified the social and historical roots of Chicana activism. Nieto Gómez was forthright in her articulation of Chicana feminism as the product of her dual positionality:

I am a Chicana feminist. I make that statement very proudly, although there is a lot of intimidation in our community and in the society in general, against people who define themselves as Chicana feminists. . . . They say you can't stand on both sides, which is a bunch of bull. . . . In fact, the statement is not contradictory at all, it is a very unified statement: I support my community and I do not ignore the women in my community.[16]

Cotera consistently produced materials that historicized the many contributions of Chicanas to fundamental issues such as equal opportunity in the workplace, access to education, and voting rights. She laid bare self-congratulatory analyses generated by mainstream feminists that assumed and asserted a cross-cultural sisterhood without acknowledging the ways in which white women were complicit in the historical subjugation of Mexican women and Chicanas:

Many Anglo women, including feminists, simply cannot accept the fact that there are minority women with brains and status. They seem unable to realize, possibly because of gross ignorance of minority history, that we have a strong history of involvement, achievement and guts, since we've had to fight not only the issue of sexism, but also the issue of racism. In terms of human dynamics, we're usually knowledgeable and aware since we are operating on two planes: the racism inherent in White-Brown relations and sexism.[17]

In the 1980s Chela Sandoval and Gloria Anzaldúa further propelled the project of redefining Chicanas' roles. In the evolution of their analyses regarding agency and its relationship to the building of alliances, Sandoval and Anzaldúa each introduced and defined the space of activism that they called respectively "oppositional consciousness" and "la conciencia mestiza."[18] The development of these concepts was key to providing critical lenses through which to view the ideological and intellectual contributions of Chicanas. A significant characteristic of both approaches is that they permit multiple and shifting positionalities within which Chicanas/os can operate. Sandoval's oppositional consciousness is the realm in which difference, contradiction, and affirmation are developed and expressed simultaneously. She argues that out of this consciousness there emerges a "methodology of the oppressed" that includes a range of theoretical and praxis-related avenues available to the disenfranchised by calling for "a poetics and politics of resistance and liberation."[19] In the space of Anzaldúa's *la conciencia mestiza,* mestizaje culture is linked with the vernacular of contemporary Chicano/a culture. Although Anzaldúa evokes the mythos of Aztec deities, she situates mestizaje as a cultural exchange that occurs within and at *la frontera,* the border. Anzaldúa constructs the border as a site of indeterminacies and calls on all people to develop "a tolerance of contradiction and of ambiguity as a strategy for survival."[20]

Women of Color: Alliances and Theories

Along with Chicana feminist expressions there flowered alliances among women of color. *This Bridge Called My Back: Writings by Radical Women of Color,* an anthology edited by the Chicana lesbian feminists Anzaldúa and Cherríe Moraga, signaled the emergence of the literary expression of the category "women of color."[21] The anthology contains a mix of genres and styles whose association insists on parallel readings of critical and creative works and whose relationships to each other prompt useful questions about the genesis of conceptual material. Alvina Quintana describes the import of this approach: "Two Chicana coeditors, ahead of their time, organized a coalition of 'women writers of color' that collectively initiated an important discussion about the politics of 'difference.'"[22] Quintana meditates on Anzaldúa and Moraga's construct of difference as the nexus of ideological organization:

> In coordinating the voices and experiences of many women writers of Color, Moraga and Anzaldúa were among the first to produce a text that contemplated critical issues concerning the relationship between linguistics, identity politics, sexuality, cultural heterogeneity, and hybridity—categories of *difference* that surpass simplistic binary paradigms.[23]

The contents of *This Bridge Called My Back* reflected an intensely critical imaginary that gave birth to a theoretical space where women of color could formulate multiple interpretations of agency and subjectivity. The book's call for cross-cultural feminist alliances established a locus for analyses that grew from the motifs created by Moraga and Anzaldúa. Anna Lowenhaupt Tsing and Chandra Talpade Mohanty are but two. Tsing looks to the category "women of color" as she outlines the parameters of a critical space that resists the conflation of the different positionalities of culturally and ethnically specific women and provides a means for "opening up the defensive boundaries of cultural nationalism."[24] Mohanty also references a strategic application found in the category "women of color" as she develops her analysis:

> What seems to constitute "women of color" or "third world women" as a viable oppositional alliance is a *common context of struggle* rather than color or racial identifications. Thus it is the common context of struggles against specific exploitative structures and systems that determines our potential political alliances.[25]

Mujeres Muralistas and Co-Madres Artistas members variously expressed their alliances with other women of color through their figurative paintings. In the case of Mujeres Muralistas, there were overt moves in their representations that linked the experiences of Chicanas/os and Latinas/os in the United States and the people of Latin America. Similarly, members of Co-Madres Artistas created artwork that evoked indigenous cultures throughout the Americas. It can be said that these creative works permitted the development of an "imagined community" between themselves and their audiences.[26] Imagined community is a concept, borrowed from Benedict Anderson, that provides a theoretical basis for understanding how alliances can be built among people who do not have ongoing personal or working relationships. Anderson specifically develops his construct to refer to illusory alliances that are created through widely dispersed media such as the newspaper or the novel. Mohanty builds on Anderson's project and situates the imagined community as a political site for women of color:

> The idea of imagined community is useful because it leads us away from essentialist notions of third world feminist struggles, suggesting political rather than biological or cultural bases for alliance. Rather, it is the way we think about race, class, and gender, the political links we choose to make among and between struggles. Thus, potentially, women of all colors (including white women) can align themselves with and participate in these imagined communities. However, clearly our relation to and centrality in particular struggles depend on our different, often conflictual, locations and histories.[27]

The artists of Mujeres Muralistas and Co-Madres Artistas created their paintings in the service of disseminating the broadest possible notion of community as applied to Latinas/os. Their works communicate the multilayered meanings of the categories "Chicana" and "women of color" and as strategic applications of imagined community. Both collectives articulated their enlarged concepts of identity through their membership as well as through their artistry. The emergence of each group signaled an ideological articulation of collectivity grounded in the expression of the artistic. For example, as a collective, Mujeres Muralistas members named themselves Chicanas, but one artist is of Venezuelan descent, another is of Guatemalan and Mexican descent, and another is of Yaqui and Mexican descent. Members of Co-Madres Artistas also identify themselves as Chicanas. Their mission statement opens with, "We, the Co-Madres Artistas, are a group of six Chicana visual artists."[28] Yet one of the members claims an unspecified indigenous ancestry and another is of European American heritage.

Unlike an imagined community, the members of each collective were known to each other, spent long hours in one another's company, and directly influenced one another's personal, artistic, and ideological choices. The application of a collective identity through their naming processes reflected practices unique to each group. Through their use of the Spanish language each group's name mirrors its connection to Chicana/o culture. According to members of Mujeres Muralistas, the artists were painting a mural when someone ventured by and asked who they were. The reply was, "Somos mujeres muralistas."[29] The artist Ralph Maradiaga, then co-director of La Galería de la Raza, encouraged them to take this description as their name, and they became Mujeres Muralistas. They did not spend time ruminating over the significance of their group's name.[30] The entrepreneurial character of the members of Co-Madres Artistas contributed to a more conscious method of naming. Members deliberately chose their name to convey a uniquely Mexican kinship among women that for them encompasses artistic support and cooperative venture. With regard to the creation of their name, they said, "The prefix co-, meaning 'together' in the English language, has been combined with the Spanish word madres (mothers) to represent our nurturing partnership."[31]

"Working with a child in one hand and a brush in the other"

"Artistic expression—literature, theater, film, dance, music, song, the visual arts—was integral to the movement as representational modes of recasting Chicana/o history and culture within the struggle for self-determination."[32] A wide range of aesthetic formulations emerged as artists became involved in the Chicana/o liberation movement. There was a blossoming of "flor y canto," public celebrations consisting of bilingual literary readings, musical and theatrical performances, and displays of visual art. Chicana/o artists were asked to create posters, handbills, and other informational materials that announced meetings, demonstrations, picket lines, lectures, and other opportunities for public discourse. Poster art demonstrated a lineage traced to the works of José Guadalupe Posada as a form of popular political commentary. Mural art emerged as a link to Mexican culture and expressly recalled the work of Los Tres Grandes. Within this tradition both art forms served as didactic visual narratives intended to prompt community dialogue on issues relating to the movement. This artwork was the product of an imaginary formulated within collective processes, and the cumulative result of this expressive energy is referred to as the Chicano Art Movement.

The poster art, drawings, and lithographs, usually announcing a community meeting or a demonstration, were most often found on telephone posts and local storefront windows, especially in those neighborhoods in the Bay Area that were home to Chicanas/os and Mexicans, such as San Francisco's Mission District and Oakland's Fruitvale District. As Chicana/o artists put their talents in the service of political and social causes, much of their art was unsigned. Malaquías Montoya recalls, "I never thought about those things as art, it was just something I did so people would pay attention to the fact that an important event was going to happen."[33] Yolanda López has a similar recollection: "The streets were my gallery . . . posters, leaflets, lapel buttons, and graphic art for neighborhood newspapers. I saw my work everywhere and unsigned."[34] When she exhibited many of these works at La Galería de la Raza in 1970, it was a surprise for many, including López, that people assumed these unattributed political images were the work of a man.[35] This expression of artistic chauvinism—that only men could create ideological inscriptions— was not unique to the incident involving López. Chicana artists, including Mujeres Muralistas, discovered that many people presumed that men created the potent images they produced. Just as those gendered tensions regarding the relationship of Chicanas to the liberation movement occurred, so they were also found in the movement of expressive culture. Alvina Quintana illustrates how the aesthetic formulations of the Chicano Movement and other U.S. Third World movements of the 1960s and 1970s reproduced the male-centered, subordinating impulses of Anglo culture:

> Nationalist aesthetic productions replicated the rhetoric that reified the suppression or omission of female experience(s). Picking up on the lessons learned from the "oppressor," African American, Asian American, Native American, and Chicano/Chicana critics legitimized "minority" cultural productions by constructing alternative literary canons that represented predominantly masculine interpretations of history, ideology, [and] culture.[36]

In a corresponding reflection, Yolanda Broyles-González critiques the reductive quality of women's theatrical representations in the dramaturgy of El Teatro Campesino:

Women's roles do not enjoy the dramatic space necessary for the unfolding of a full character. In their confinement, women do not evolve beyond a single dimension. With the exception of *La Virgen de Tepeyac*, all Teatro Campesino plays have males as their focus. The female figures are those *affected* by men; they are peripheral, the ones to whom things happen.[37]

Given the historical relationship between the United Farm Workers Union (UFW) and El Teatro Campesino, it is deeply ironic that the theater group would stray so far from Chávez's egalitarian methodologies. On the matter of Chicana/o aesthetic expression, Chávez was, as always, unique among the leadership of the Chicano Movement. United Farm Worker actions, whether pilgrimage, picket line, informational table, meeting, or prayer vigil, included an image of La Virgen de Guadalupe.[38] For some, "La Virgen symbolized the Mexico of the poor and the humble."[39] The equally omnipresent flag of the UFW, with its black eagle encircled in white on a red background, hearkened to the colors of flags carried during strikes in Mexico.[40] These same colors might also be said to evoke the "Land of Black and Red," Tlillan-Tlapallan, the ancestral home of Quetzalcoatl's mother.[41] These visual representations conjured a legendary past that linked the Mexican heritage of many migrant workers; but the images differed greatly from those artistic expressions that glorified Chicano history as an exclusively male narrative. The unproblematized presentation of a Chicano aesthetic resulted in the enduring signification of Chicanas as subordinated agents within the movement. Shifra Goldman and Tomás Ybarra-Frausto describe the circulation and operation of one such representation:

One of the most ubiquitous images in Chicano art (derived from Mexican calendars) has been the sexy, often seminude figure of the Aztec princess from the Iztaccihuatl/Popocatépetl legend, carried "Tarzan-Jane" fashion by a gloriously arrayed warrior prince. This rendition epitomizes the notion of the passive woman protected by the active man.[42]

Paradoxically, these traditional roles have emerged as a source of ideological reflection for many Chicana artists, including the members of Mujeres Muralistas and Co-Madres Artistas.[43] Both collectives frequently depicted the foundational elements of the movement, mestizaje and the family, but subverted the commonly circulated articulations by presenting transgressive formulations. An early observation by Sybil Venegas identifies the representational distinctions that marked the wall art of Mujeres Muralistas as unique:

> Bold, colorful, figurative and in harmony with nature, the murals of las Mujeres Muralistas reflect life in Latin American culture. Women and children are a topic of focus, while general themes are concerned with nature, plants and animals, in attempts to provide the people in the Mission with alternative natural environments in the midst of their man-made urban metropolis.[44]

Operating under social and cultural expectations to maintain the domestic sphere, seek gainful employment, and contribute meaningfully to community affairs, there is little time for Chicana artists to create art. As one Chicana artist quips, "All of my work is done with a child in one hand, a brush in the other."[45] The artists of Mujeres Muralistas were able, to varying degrees, to maintain a high level of artistic production even as they engaged in this multitude of tasks. Co-Madres Artistas members chose to defer their focus as artists until after their children were grown, their positions were secured in the workplace, and their commitment to community was well established. Instead of suspending their artistic production altogether, the Co-Madres Artistas artists moderated their creative output in order to meet their other responsibilities and remain active. Arts administrator Theresa Harlan situates Co-Madres Artistas' ongoing service to their families, community, and the arts as they traveled their paths to creative expression:

> Like many communities all over the United States and the world there are collectives of artists, doers, creators, and community organizers who work committedly [sic] for their communities and the empowerment of those communities. Many times self-empowerment is placed aside for the needs of the community. Co-Madres Artistas is such a group. . . . Historically women of many communities donate time and services with little recognition for their own interests and needs. The difficulty of making time for developing one's individual art making is often restrained because of family demands and needs.[46]

Goldman and Ybarra-Frausto underscore the social obstacles facing Chicanas who elect to become artists:

For women, simply becoming artists frequently involved breaking stereotypes within the patriarchal family (or working class family that conceived no economic advantage to be derived from entering the arts); persisting within the educational system, especially in opposition to its insistence "on mainstream" culture and art forms; juggling duties as lovers, wives, mothers, and workers with time for creative work; and finally being sufficiently self-confident and assertive to obtain exhibition space or commissions.[47]

Venegas outlines the circumstances requisite to the development and maturation of artists:

Education, training and apprenticeship clearly a prerequisite of an artist for the acquisition of necessary skills was generally not available until the turn of the century for the Anglo woman, the middle of the 20th Century for the Chicano and only until very recently for the Chicana.[48]

Chicanas, as well as other artists of color, are challenged to find mentors in higher education who understand artistry that emerges from traditions other than mainstream white culture.[49] As noted, all members of both collectives attended college; this fact was an important source of their success as artists. College provided the developing artists with foundational skills, and it also was where they met each other. Some of the artists were fortunate to find mentors: Irma Lerma Barbosa of Co-Madres Artistas was enabled by a master artist, Tarmo Pasto, who was not of Mexican descent; Ester Hernández, Irene Pérez, and Patricia Rodríguez of Mujeres Muralistas received early lessons from Malaquías Montoya at his Taller de Artes Graphicas.

Ana Castillo illustrates with dramatic inflection how some Chicanas are unable to overcome the paucity of support and the social pressures they face for their gender role transgressions: "Many women who showed great creative promise did not continue. Some were forced to stop. Some went mad. Others died."[50] Although there were struggles around the sexual politics of the Chicano Art Movement, Chicanas were provided with some measure of encouragement, as well as opportunities for direct engagement.

The Chicana artists in this narrative, the women of Mujeres Muralistas and Co-Madres Artistas, affiliated with different aspects of the Chicano Movement as student activists advocating on behalf of equal opportunity and access, through affinity work with the UFW, by engaging in the antiwar effort. The holistic melding of their creative talent and social consciousness resulted in artwork that functioned as a form of critical reflection. Angela Y. Davis describes how this approach to artistic production results in a didactic formulation:

> Art is a form of social consciousness—a special form of social con-sciousness that can potentially awaken an urge in those affected by it to creatively transform their oppressive environments. Progressive art can assist people to learn not only about objective forces at work in the society in which they live, but also about the intensely social character of their interior lives.[51]

In a parallel conceptual move Anzaldúa depicts self-definition and resistance as the unified products of artistic expression:

> Art is about identity, among other things, and creativity is political. Creative acts are forms of political activism employing definite aes-thetic strategies for resisting dominant cultural norms and are not merely aesthetic exercises. We build culture as we inscribe in these various forms.[52]

Davis and Anzaldúa are not explicitly describing the work and processes of Mujeres Muralistas and Co-Madres Artistas, but their analyses reflect the social impact of the art of the two collectives. Both groups consistently painted works that commented on the many different cultures and tradi-tions that existed in the Chicana/o community. Their murals and easel paintings portrayed people in settings that were readily recognizable to their Chicana/o audiences. Venegas describes this hybridized process:

> As an art form, Chicana art is just beginning. Like Chicano art, it attempts to define Chicano identity within the larger framework of social change. However, more specifically, the Chicana artist seeks to establish her identity as a woman and also as a Chicana. Thus the Chicana artist is often concerned with the woman and her struggle; her artwork ultimately reflective of life rendering messages and

challenging commentaries on the Chicana in efforts to come to grips with her current, changing situation.[53]

While the artists of Mujeres Muralistas and Co-Madres Artistas strongly identified with the Chicano Art Movement, they did not conform their images of themselves or other Chicanas to fit its prevailing sexism. Correspondingly, the women of these collectives did not call themselves feminists, yet their self-identification as artists clearly situated them as women operating outside of traditional constructs. In subsequent chapters, we learn from collective members how they negotiated the social and cultural terrain in their journeys as Chicana artists.

Notes

1. Shifra Goldman and Tomás Ybarra-Frausto, *Arte Chicano: A Comprehensive Annotated Bibliography of Chicano Art, 1965–1981* (Berkeley: Chicano Studies Library Publications Unit, University of California, 1985), 52–55.
2. Eva Sperling Cockcroft and Holly Barnet-Sánchez, eds., *Signs from the Heart: California Chicano Murals* (Albuquerque: University of New Mexico Press, 1993), 14.
3. Raymond Williams, *Problems in Materialism and Culture: Selected Essays* (London: Verso Press, 1980), 41.
4. Ibid.
5. Alma M. García, ed., *Chicana Feminist Thought: The Basic Historical Writings* (New York: Routledge, 1997), 1.
6. Yolanda Broyles-González, *El Teatro Campesino: Theater in the Chicano Movement* (Austin: University of Texas Press, 1994), 140.
7. García, *Chicana Feminist Thought,* 2.
8. For an early example of this construct, see "La Plebe," in *Aztlán: An Anthology of Mexican American Literature,* ed. Luis Váldez and Stan Steiner (New York: Alfred A. Knopf, 1972), xiii–xxxiv.
9. For an eloquent historical analysis of the ways in which *carnal* and *chingón* came to signify male-centered manifestations of leadership within the Chicano Movement, see Elizabeth Martínez, "Chingón Politics Die Hard," *Z Magazine* (April 1990).
10. César E. Chávez, "El Plan de Delano," *El Malcriado,* March 17, 1966.
11. See Peter Matthiessen, *Sal Si Puedes: César Chávez and the New American Revolution* (New York: Dell Publishing Co., 1969).
12. Ana Nieto-Gómez, "La Feminista," *Encuentro Feminil* 1, no. 2 (1974): 34.
13. For an impressive array of early Chicana feminist theory and strategy, see Garcia's *Chicana Feminist Thought.*
14. Enriqueta Longeaux Vasquez, "¡Despierten Hermanas! The Women of La Raza—Part II," *El Grito del Norte* 2, no. 10 (1969): 3. Emphasis in original.
15. Marta Cotera, *Diosa y Hembra: The History and Heritage of Chicanas in the U.S.* (Austin: Information Systems Development, 1976).

16. Ana Nieto Gómez, "Chicana Feminism," *Caracol* 2, no. 5 (1976): 3.
17. Marta Cotera, "Among the Feminists: Racist, Classist Issues—1976," *The Chicana Feminist* (Austin: Information Systems Development, 1977), 44.
18. Chela Sandoval, "U.S. Third World Feminism: The Theory and Method of Oppositional Consciousness in the Postmodern World," *Genders* 10 (spring 1991); Gloria Anzaldúa, *Borderlands/La Frontera: The New Mestiza* (San Francisco: Spinsters/Aunt Lute, 1987).
19. Sandoval, "U.S. Third World Feminism," 256.
20. Anzaldúa, *Borderlands/La Frontera,* 62.
21. Cherríe Moraga and Gloria Anzaldúa, eds., *This Bridge Called My Back: Writings by Radical Women of Color* (New York: Kitchen Table: Women of Color Press, 1983). A manuscript of mine, "Feminist Literary Contributions of Gloria Anzaldúa and Cherríe Moraga," presented at the First International MELUS Conference held at the University of Hawai'i, Manoa, in 1997, details the ways in which the publication of *This Bridge* provided new sites of social agency and literary expression among women of color.
22. Alvina E. Quintana, *Home Girls: Chicana Literary Voices* (Philadelphia: Temple University Press, 1996), 140.
23. Ibid., 115. Emphasis in original.
24. Anna Lowenhaupt Tsing, *In the Realm of the Diamond Queen: Marginality in an Out of the Way Place* (Princeton, N.J.: Princeton University Press, 1993), 18.
25. Chandra Talpade Mohanty, "Cartographies of Struggle: Third World Women and the Politics of Feminism," in *Third World Women and the Politics of Feminism,* ed. Chandra Talpade Mohanty, Ann Russo, and Lourdes Torres (Bloomington: Indiana University Press, 1991), 7. Emphasis in original
26. Benedict Anderson, *Imagined Communities: Reflections on the Origin and Spread of Nationalism* (London: Verso Press, 1983). Imagined community is a construct loosely borrowed from the work of Anderson, who posits that the rise of the nation-state can be seen, in part, as a result of the emergence of the newspaper and the novel as nineteenth-century genres of mass communication. He describes how widespread media distribution allows for individuals to obtain information about one another, in spite of the fact that they do not personally know one another. Anderson argues that the novel, through the literary device of simultaneity, makes it possible for people to imagine others as though in alliance. This alliance is built on a sense of belonging, which he calls "horizontal comradeship."
27. Mohanty, "Cartographies of Struggle," 4.
28. *Co-Madres Artistas: Story/Visions from the Cactus Tree: A Catalogue of Fine Art* (Sacramento: California Arts Council, 1994), 2.
29. Irene Pérez, interview, September 20, 1993; Ester Hernández, interview, September 17, 1993.
30. Irene Pérez, interview, September 20, 1993; Ester Hernández, interview, September 17, 1993.
31. "Co-Madres Artistas," in *Art Catalogue for the Fifth Annual Latina Leadership Network Conference* (1992).
32. Goldman and Ybarra-Frausto, *Arte Chicano,* 32.
33. Malaquías Montoya, interview, October 4, 1994.
34. Betty LaDuke, *Women Artists: Multi-Cultural Visions* (Trenton: Red Sea Press, 1992), 104.

35. Ibid.
36. Quintana, *Home Girls*, 19–20.
37. Broyles-González, *El Teatro Campesino*, 136. Emphasis in original.
38. Patricia Zavella deserves thanks for directing me to the scholarship of John Hammerback, whose rhetorical analyses of Chávez's oratory is invaluable. John C. Hammerback, Richard J. Jensen, and José Ángel Gutiérrez, *A War of Words: Chicano Protest in the 1960s and 1970s* (Westport, Conn.: Greenwood Press, 1985).
39. John Gregory Dunne, *Delano,* rev. ed. (New York: Noonday Press, 1971), 132.
40. John C. Hammerback and Richard J. Jensen, *The Rhetorical Career of César Chávez* (College Station: Texas A&M University Press, 1998), 39.
41. Miguel Covarrubias, *Indian Art of Mexico and Central America* (New York: Alfred A. Knopf, 1957), 268.
42. Goldman and Ybarra-Frausto, *Arte Chicano,* 43.
43. Such imagery is found in the work of Ester Hernández, Yolanda López, Delilah Montoya, Barbara Carrasco, Maya Christina González, and Juana Alicia, to name a few.
44. Sybil Venegas, "The Artists and Their Work: The Role of the Chicana Artist," *ChisméArte* 1, no. 4 (1977): 5.
45. Sybil Venegas, "Conditions for Producing Chicana Art," *ChisméArte* 1, no. 4 (1977): 3.
46. Theresa Harlan, "Co-Madres Artistas: Making a Name for Self and Community," in *Co-Madres Artistas: Story/Visions,* 3.
47. Goldman and Ybarra-Frausto, *Arte Chicano,* 42.
48. Venegas, "Conditions for Producing Chicana Art," 3.
49. One example of this insidious process of institutionalized racism can be seen in the personal history of Yolanda López. In 1973 López was a graduate student in the master's program at the University of California, San Diego. On viewing her body of work and its distinctly Chicana-based imagery, López's teacher commented, "Ethnic art is dead, corny and a rehash." Years later as she reflected on that moment, López commented on the one-way nature of the artistic dialogue that occurred between herself and Anglo audiences: "I spoke their language, but they wouldn't bother to learn mine." LaDuke, *Women Artists,* 104.
50. Ana Castillo, "Feminist Visions," *Crossroads Magazine,* May 1993, 9.
51. Angela Y. Davis, *Women, Culture, and Politics* (New York: Vintage Books, 1989), 199.
52. Gloria Anzaldúa, *Haciendo Caras: Making Face, Making Soul, Creative and Critical Perspectives by Feminists of Color* (San Francisco: Aunt Lute Foundation, 1990), xxiv.
53. Venegas, "The Artists and Their Work," 5.

TWO

Mujeres Muralistas

"We Offer You Colors We Make"

A mural is a painting . . . done by people who want to put art where it belongs: with the people, in the streets around us in our daily lives. Our interest as artists is to put art close to where it needs to be. Close to children; close to old people; close to everyone who has to walk or ride the buses. . . . We want our art out in the streets or in places where a lot of people go each day, the hospitals, health centers, clinics, restaurants, and other public places. . . . Walls with rainbow colors from people with rainbow minds. . . . We offer you colors we make.[1]

Historical narratives on Mujeres Muralistas characterize the group as a changing constellation of artists whose work was done over several years.[2] I am interested in the period between 1973 and 1975, when the core artists Graciela Carrillo, Irene Pérez, and Patricia Rodríguez created murals on Balmy Alley, then joined with Consuelo Méndez to paint *Latinoamerica, Para el Mercado,* and *Rhomboidal Parallelogram;* Carrillo, Pérez, and Rodríguez then painted *Fantasy World for Children.* After this, other artists worked on mural projects under the name Mujeres Muralistas. I selected these four murals as the locus of discussion because they are the most sharply delineated in terms of the artists' creative and social approaches. A close reading of the representational elements of *Latinoamerica* is also presented because it was the germinal cooperative venture for the collective: it profoundly determined the working relationship and visual elements of the three subsequent murals painted by this configuration of Mujeres Muralistas.

This chapter is informed by interviews with three of the four core artists, Consuelo Méndez, Irene Pérez, and Patricia Rodríguez, as well as one of the assistants, Ester Hernández. Throughout their history as a collective Mujeres Muralistas painted in the tradition of the *maestras,* more experienced artists who trained emergent artists whom they called assistants. All the artists are alternately referred to as muralists or *muralistas,* although their abilities and interests encompassed a wider range of creative expression than is indicated by the use of these terms. They were then and are now prolific artists working in a variety of forms, including painting, lithography, installation, performance, and multimedia.

Mural painting requires a tremendous amount of work.[3] To describe the process as complex is to grossly understate the level of negotiation and diplomacy necessary to create wall art. The technical logistics and representational concerns of mural painting, compounded by the nuanced personal interactions among the artists, contribute to an ever-widening series of communicative processes. Add to these interactions those that take place between the artists and the community or group interested in having a mural in their midst. Another layer is the ongoing commentary as audiences respond to the mural and communicate their likes and dislikes, concerns for accuracy of detail, and suggestions or additions to the work. This response and analysis is sustained from the early stages of conceptualization through the design and painting processes and, of course, in narratives such as this that take place decades after the work of art has ceased to exist. (The longevity of murals, it seems, is in inverse proportion to the analyses of their presentation and representation.)

In addition to the overlapping dialogue that takes place in the creation of a mural, the artists must undertake logistical planning and practical implementation. This work includes assembling and disassembling scaffolding, and climbing up, down, and across the scaffolding while carrying paints, brushes, cleaning cloths, and other paraphernalia. Working in all weather conditions adds to the rigor of mural painting; the work goes on under hot sun, in fog, and against the chill of wind. After such an arduous undertaking, it is fitting that most murals are welcomed into being with ritual celebrations that include the requisite ingredients of food, music, dancing, and an invocation or blessing. Such was the multileveled work that awaited the young Chicanas studying art in San Francisco during the early 1970s who would become the Mujeres Muralistas.

Of Manifestos and Muralistas

A quotation from the 1974 manifesto issued by Mujeres Muralistas, drafted after the completion of their first mural, *Latinoamerica*, introduces this chapter. It is a plainly articulated statement about the public nature of their art and their vital relationship to their audiences. Mujeres Muralistas' declaration is a text whose simplicity masks the interactions through which it was created and disseminated. The manifesto is cited in the writings of art historians and journalists and referred to as a collectively produced aesthetic pronouncement.[4]

According to Ester Hernández, each of the artists had her own political philosophy, and the statement was not an assertion of collective goals but primarily expressed one member's ideology. Hernández's view is that there were many differences among the group's participants, such as ethnicity, political consciousness, class background, and sexual orientation, as well as artistic ability and interest, which were sometimes sources of dissonance among the artists. However, these dissimilarities did not diminish their commitment to working as artists in the service of the Chicana/o community. As Hernández points out:

> We didn't have all of that philosophical-ideological stuff like Consuelo [Méndez]. When they finished that first mural, she was the one who actually put out the whole manifesto. So then people began to think of us in that way, although we weren't necessarily political. Some of us didn't have that kind of real heavy political thing, even though we considered ourselves artists of the Movimiento. Our artistic abilities were in different stages. But we all, in different degrees, wanted to do something for our community with our art.[5]

Irene Pérez, Patricia Rodríguez, and Consuelo Méndez herself did not dispute the assertion that Méndez was primarily responsible for the creation of the manifesto.[6] Méndez characterizes the statement as follows:

> [It was a] way for us to make an overt connection to the mural move-ment of Mexico. The manifesto was written to resonate with the 1924 manifesto issued by David Alfaro Siqueros and El Sindicato de Pintores y Escultores. It was our way of making our politics known.[7]

In addition to Méndez's self-appointed political role, another of the founding artists, Patricia Rodríguez, assumed the role of public spokesperson on behalf of the group. Pérez describes how Rodríguez came into this position:

> Patricia kind of took it upon herself to be a spokesperson for us. She used "we" a lot, and some of us had a hard time with that. Patricia was very verbal. She was the articulate person who always talked with the media. So, oftentimes, it was her point of view that was expounded in the media.[8]

By all accounts, Rodríguez easily communicated with members of the media and had a flair for positioning the group's work. She says of her role:

> It was important to bring our work to the attention of the public. I wanted to help in doing that. I felt comfortable in doing that. In addition to being an artist, everyone brought a different strength to the group. Mine was the ability to present our work to the public.[9]

By providing a public face for Mujeres Muralistas, Méndez and Rodríguez gave the group a perceived organizational quality of fixity that was absent in the actual practices of the artists. Primarily as a result of the economic exigencies of studying and working as artists, the internal organization of Mujeres Muralistas was always in flux. The artists of the core group, Carrillo, Méndez, Pérez, and Rodríguez, altered their involvement, responsibilities, and tasks from one mural to the next. The variability of their roles meant that their working relationships to one another changed from project to project. In addition, their interactions were subject to pressures brought on by scarce resources, the high level of detail attendant to mural work, the availability and interests of participant artists, and the skills each artist brought to the group.

These details, hidden behind the seamless solidarity of the manifesto, are interesting because they speak to how the artists respected the boundaries of their individual artistic skills even as each asserted her position within the group. Their eclectic style of working out individualized social locations and creative approaches as they created the unified expression of a mural evokes Chela Sandoval's concept "differential oppositional consciousness":

This dialectical modulation between forms of consciousness permits functioning within, yet beyond, the demands of dominant ideology: the practitioner breaks with ideology while also speaking in and from within ideology. The differential form of oppositional consciousness thus is composed of narrative worked self-consciously. Its processes generate the other story—the counterpoise.[10]

As is evident from the interviews, the artists of Mujeres Muralistas clearly introjected one another's consciousness, and what emerged for each artist was a more clearly differentiated articulation of her creative approach and social identity as a Chicana artist. The members of Mujeres Muralistas created a space in which their heterogeneity was not reduced to a polarized expression of static tension but became a site where difference could operate as the foundation for cooperative venture and mutual support in the development of Chicana artistic expression. The collective processes of Mujeres Muralistas recall Audre Lorde's description of the ways in which difference serves as a useful tool for asserting collective power:

> Within the interdependence of mutual (non-dominant) differences lies that security which enables us to descend into the chaos of knowledge and return with true visions of our future, along with the concomitant power to effect those changes which can bring that future into being. Difference is that raw and powerful connection from which our personal power is forged.[11]

The manifesto's concluding language, "We offer you colors we make," deserves attention because it conjures the Mexican tradition of *la ofrenda*, a site-specific collection of objects reminiscent of beloved ones, now deceased. At first glance, the relationship between the art form of the altar—the altar-installation—and the mural might not seem apparent, but there are connections.[12] As works of art, each of the genres shares an evanescent quality; each is vulnerable to dismantling, defacing, or razing. Their ephemeral positioning as works of public art serves to further underscore their resemblance as presentation. Although different in terms of genre, the altar-installation and the mural can be said to operate as analogous representational forms, in that they are expressive sites of remembrance, discovery, and volition that can be located within Chicana/o cultural tradition.

Tomás Ybarra-Frausto describes the development of Chicana/o artistic practices as a three-part process with the following trajectory: the retrieval of Mexican traditions, the transformation of these traditions into hybridized Chicana/o expressions, and the emergence of a reconfigured, expanded cultural movement that borrows from and shares with other subaltern traditions.[13] In these specific instances, both art forms, the altar-installation and the mural, spring from Mexican customs of public creative expression, each has undergone changes of translation in the context of El Norte, and both genres have moved beyond their roots in the Chicana/o community and have been adapted and modified by disparate populations, many of whom also have altar traditions, for example, Africans, Asians, Native Americans, and Middle Easterners.[14]

Beginnings and Influences

An insistent mural tradition has asserted itself on the exteriors and interiors of Oakland–San Francisco Bay Area architecture since Diego Rivera's stay in the 1930s. The city of San Francisco is said to support the highest per capita mural output in the world.[15] A map of mural sites in the Mission District shows that at the time of its publication in 1993, there were no fewer than sixty-five locations of wall art in a twenty-seven-block area. The actual number of individual murals in the area is far larger, for many of these sites contained several murals.[16]

Balmy Alley, located off of Army Street between Twenty-fourth and Twenty-fifth Streets, is one of those locations. The street is a monument to the variety of form and content, as well as the longevity, of the Bay Area mural movement. From 1973 to the present, every building facing onto this one-block-long street has been the site of a mural. Some of the original murals have been restored, while others have been painted over to make way for new murals. Some of the Bay Area's most prolific artists have created murals on this street: Juana Alicia, Ray Patlán, Susan Kelk Cervantes, Brooke Francher, Miranda Bergman, Osha Neuman, Carlos Loarca, and Xochitl Nevel-Guerrero, among many others.

The Balmy Alley murals were begun in 1973 as an after-school program for children, who painted the first murals.[17] The director of the program also invited adult artists to participate. Three of the four founding artists of Mujeres Muralistas, Irene Pérez, Graciela Carrillo, and Patricia Rodríguez, painted untitled works. Carrillo and Rodríguez had each painted murals before their work together on Balmy Alley.[18] For Pérez, it was the first venture into mural art:

> It was actually the first time that I did a mural on a wall. It was an experience that I did on my own. It was a hard one. It was a tough one because I didn't have the scaffolding. I had to work on a ladder. It was also very difficult because none of us were being paid. But everybody felt committed to doing some artwork for the community.[19]

These murals serve as early indicators of the representations and processes that would later emerge from the collective. Pérez's wall art fills a small horizontal space in a gable that hangs over a dual-garage-door opening. Two young Latinos, dressed in lavender, light blue, and white campesino clothing, play wood flutes as they sit back to back. The young people foreground two flat planes of dark and light blue, whose pulsing waves of color seem to rise as music from their flutes.

Carrillo and Rodríguez's mural spans a large two-story space of a garage front. The scene is a jungle-underwater setting where lush green foliage frames a circle of blue sky and aqua water. The upper portion of the ringed space depicts an above-water scenario with a muted yellow sun surrounded by clouds, birds, and tree branches. The branches move down into the oceanscape and become underwater vegetation with phantasmal swimming fish. The bottom of the circle, the sea floor, is visually anchored by vegetation growing up from the jungle flora and into the ocean.

Although Carrillo and Rodríguez had worked together previously, the two artists made little attempt to mesh their styles in creating this mural. It is clear that the jungle was painted by one and the oceanscape by another. The artists' approach to painting the wall art of Balmy Alley was an early manifestation of Mujeres Muralistas' later practice of mixing individual styles in a cooperative effort. While the scale of mural work required that the artists collaborate on content, there was seemingly little attempt to develop a singular style that served to characterize the group's work. The murals of Mujeres Muralistas were, however, marked by a well-defined representational context, in which the content revolved around a common theme. Subject matter that unified their later work included Latin American culture depicted through everyday occurrences such as the playing of music and dancing, agrarian work, interactions at the marketplace, and domestic life.

In part, this eclectic quality may have emerged from the varied artistic experiences that each artist brought to the group effort. The processes necessary to enact a hybridized style required too much energy and time from the artists, who were always working against a deadline as they simultaneously handled the creative as well as the logistical aspects of mural work. None of the artists interviewed for this study was able to explain why the group did not develop a common style. But they each stated that at the time it seemed the most democratic to divide a mural into sections and assign each artist a portion of the wall.

Two useful effects resulted from this approach. All of the works—*Latinoamerica, Para el Mercado, Rhomboidal Parallelogram,* and *Fantasy World for Children*—had themes that emphasized the heterogeneity of the Latina/o experience, and the mixing of individual artistic styles enhanced the group's vision of cultural diversity. By choosing to portray the different aspects of Latin American culture, the artists were able to draw on their varied life experiences and backgrounds. Hernández grew up in rural California in a family of farmworkers and since the 1970s has been involved with the United Farm Workers Union.[20] Pérez is a native of East Oakland with strong ties to the neighborhood's predominantly Latina/o and African American community. Méndez, the daughter of a physician, emigrated from Venezuela to the United States to attend college. Rodríguez, born and raised in Texas, came to the Bay Area to attend college.

Another result of assigning different sections of the mural to specific artists was that the experienced muralistas were able to assist those with less hands-on knowledge without commanding the entire effort. In 1977 Sybil Venegas wrote of the painting that emerged from their varied experiences as individual artists: "Though las Muralistas collectively portray a style in their murals, they are also individual artists working in various media other than murals."[21] At the time, Pérez, Carrillo, Rodríguez, and Méndez were students at the San Francisco Art Institute, where they worked in a variety of media. Hernández first studied creative writing and then art at the University of California, Berkeley. Malaquías Montoya, a muralist and silkscreen artist, recalled that Pérez, Rodríguez, and Hernández also studied at the East Oakland graphics workshop he founded and coordinated, where he taught them silkscreen and poster art techniques.[22]

Involvement in community art-related projects was a common thread among the artists. Méndez painted murals in a neighborhood recreation center and a children's center, while Hernández designed posters for community events and organizing efforts. Pérez painted several murals at

East Bay schools and clinics, and Carrillo and Rodríguez worked with groups of young people. In addition, the artists were involved to varying degrees with the then emergent Galería de la Raza.

In 1974 a commission from the Model Cities Program for their Mission District office provided both the opportunity and the funding for the artists who would form Mujeres Muralistas. The exterior concrete wall offered as the site for the wall art presented the group with challenges and possibilities. The wall ran the length of a building, facing on a flat, open parking lot, which was visible to people traveling along the street, parallel to the lot. Its concrete surface was fairly free of intrusive architectural elements, save for one security light, the conduit for the light, and a red gasoline pump that was anchored in the pavement of the parking lot and intruded visually into the central portion of the space.

Méndez was the artist initially contacted to paint the wall. Although she had worked alone on a number of murals, the scale of the site for this project, seventy-six feet horizontally and twenty-six feet vertically, was impressive. She asked artists whose talents she knew to join her. In addition to herself, the coordinating muralistas for *Latinoamerica* were Carrillo, Rodríguez, and Pérez. Four others, including Hernández, worked as assistants on this mural.[23] Méndez recalls, "It was a huge wall, larger than any of us had worked on, and we were going to be paid! There weren't many paid jobs for artists, and we were trying to get what we could. So naturally we were excited."[24]

The planning and painting of this mural would stand distinct from subsequent wall art projects by Mujeres Muralistas because of the time spent researching and discussing its content, form, and style. Rodríguez's downstairs garage on Balmy Alley became their office. She remembers, "Everybody had a key to my home. The downstairs garage was the workplace."[25] The core artists spent several months planning their approach. One of the people with whom they consulted was Emmy Lou Packard, an artist who had worked with Diego Rivera. Pérez recollects:

> She had painted the mural at Coit Tower. [At the time,] she was living in the Mission, and still had a studio. She was very helpful. We consulted with her, and she told us a lot about the technical stuff and about working together as a group. It was exciting to have a historical connection with somebody who worked with Rivera![26]

Pérez also remembers that in their discussions they had firm ideas about the content of their prospective mural:

Initially, we talked about a lot of different things. I guess you could say we brainstormed. We wanted a mural that was not done like a lot of the men had been doing. A lot of the heavy-duty political blood and guts, police-coming-down-on-the-people stuff. We wanted to do something that showed more the positive aspects of our culture: the music, food, things that had not been seen in other murals. We wanted to do something positive.[27]

Although the artists were interested in participating in a joint effort, they nonetheless worked out their design concepts separately. In fact, from the beginning, the mural was intended to be developed as a whole that would emerge from its various parts. This approach seemed to challenge rather than ignore the artists' practice of collaboration, as Pérez relates:

Everyone took on a different section and drew out different things on separate pieces of graph paper. It was from this that we worked a composition out. I think that I had little bit more to do with the composition part because Consuelo, Patricia, and Graciela were kind of overwhelmed with other things. But it was great, and lots of energy was exchanged. Everybody kept their own styles, but it worked out.[28]

Rodríguez also remembers that they each marveled at the relative ease with which they worked on this project:

One of the things that was magical was how well we worked together. Here we were working on a space, a canvas, and a canvas is a very private thing, and we were able to share that intimate space, affirm each other, and paint in our particular styles.[29]

The group chose not to designate a leader. Some of the artists believe that this decision gave them an organizational vigor. Rodríguez says, "I think we were a vital group because we had no leader."[30] Hernández shares Rodríguez's recollection of the excitement of working together, in spite of the meager financial rewards: "There was about $1,000 to cover materials and salaries. We would have been better off working in a tortilla factory. But we learned a lot."[31]

Pérez remembers that the organizational work surrounding *Latinoamerica* was filled with details, and although the artists did not assign one another to specific tasks, the different responsibilities were handled, in large measure, because of the enthusiasm that each artist brought to the work:

> Because we wanted to do something positive, that in itself was a good start. Consuelo was responsible for getting the money. Someone else ran out and got the paint. Everybody did different things. The scaffolding needed to be put together. Somehow it just worked out.[32]

Rodríguez recalls that the work provided them with a deeper understanding of their relationship to one another: "It was the first time that Latinas were working together as artists on projects, and we focused on the struggles of La Mujer."[33] For Hernández, the rigorous physicality of mural work was an extension of her family's experiences as farmworkers and not, as it was for some, an attempt to make a feminist statement about the abilities of Chicanas:[34]

> Physically, it was real demanding work, and a lot of people were impressed that we would just march up and down the scaffolding. But, you know, a lot of us in the group came from families with real strong and independent women. It wasn't that we had to prove that women are strong. Come on! We had our mothers, our tías [aunts], women who were farmworkers, who were used to working in the fields, filling and lugging forty-pound loads. We really weren't trying to do the whole feminist thing. Even though that's how they wrote about it, it wasn't true. We already knew our own strength.[35]

Regardless of the group's intentions concerning feminist practices or concepts, by virtue of their wholly nontraditional work environment, the effect of their public actions, as the Chicanas clambered across scaffolding with buckets and brushes, projected a feminist statement. As Amalia Mesa-Bains points out:

> Circumscribing public space was rarely associated with the work of women and Las Mujeres Muralistas was a revolutionary effort. Their

structure resembled that of other organizations in the Movement whose work was publicly accessible, anti-elitist, and collective in nature. Their formula was feminist.[36]

Pérez remembers that passersby unaccustomed to seeing women, particularly Chicanas, climbing and working on scaffolding just assumed they were men:

> People would see us from the street, the sidewalk. They thought they were seeing men painting a mural, until we came down, and they came up to talk to us. Then they said, "Wow! We thought you guys were guys!" Even the photographer who owned a store [across from the mural site] . . . came over and took pictures of us working. He said he could have sworn that what he saw were men painting. People were really surprised to see that we were actually women.[37]

Hernández recalls public reaction in an equally dramatic fashion: "People [practically] had heart attacks! Most of us were small and short. We weren't big women, but the wall was big! That's why people were surprised when they saw us up close."[38]

Chicano muralists dropped by their site from time to time to offer unsolicited assistance and words of advice. As Hernández recalls:

> A couple of the guys doing murals out there came around now and then to offer their help. But we would just kind of tease them or joke with them. We weren't into fighting or trying to run their asses out of our area. We didn't really do that confrontational type of stuff. The weak men were intimidated, and the strong men, the men who were sure of themselves and their worth, didn't feel threatened. They were very supportive. Fortunately, I would say the really important people, the men who were really leaders, like Rene Yañez, Rupert García, and Malaquías Montoya, were very open and helpful. They were smart enough to realize that we were making a special, much needed contribution.[39]

Pérez remembers that in addition to the support they received from these Chicano artists, they received encouragement from Ralph Maradiaga. At the time, Maradiaga was codirector of La Galería de la Raza. Pérez's brother-in-law, Michael Ríos, a muralist in San Francisco, also became supportive of the Chicanas' mural work and was influenced by it, although he was critical initially. Pérez describes Ríos's artistic transformation:

> At first, he said, "You aren't using sophisticated colors. You're using very bright, vibrant colors." I said, "Forget you, man! These are the colors we want to paint." Basically, he felt that sophisticated colors were a lot of dark shades and a lot of blacks. We kept saying, "Ahh, those colors are too dark." Depressing colors, you know? We had an influence there. He started to come around on the use of colors. His murals began to be a little more cultural rather than totally political.[40]

It is also possible that the criticism arose from envy. During the early 1970s, contemporary wall art was still emerging in the Bay Area and there were few commissions for murals. (It is interesting that two of the largest murals commissioned in the Bay Area, *Latinoamerica* and *Maestrapeace*, were painted by collectives composed entirely of women. *Maestrapeace*, created in the early 1990s, was painted on the four-story San Francisco Women's Building structure by a collective who eventually took as their name the name of the mural. Pérez was a core artist on both murals.) However, it also seems that Mujeres Muralistas were criticized because their portrayals of culturally affirming themes emerged from the everyday lives of Chicanos/as and successfully contested Chicano nationalist representations valorizing the depiction of heroes and epic struggles. Hernández describes Mujeres Muralistas' imagery and its development in this way:

> We were looking beyond ourselves, to our children, to the elderly, to the future. We were concerned with what was around us. We had the general feeling that men chose to deal with themes of social change through the portrayal of violence, heroes, and the glories of the past. In those days [the 1970s], they [the artistic representations] were all Aztec princes and Zapatistas. As a group of women, we wanted to go in another direction with our images.[41]

Timothy W. Drescher, an art historian, describes the significance of portraying the quotidian as he comments on the value of visual representations such as are found in *Latinoamerica*:

> The work, as with many community murals, takes on a didactic function, educating its audience about the diversity of Latino influences

in the Mission District. For passersby already aware of the references, a specific image can be a warm reminder of childhood in a distant homeland.[42]

In spite of the criticisms leveled at their work by some Chicano artists, Mujeres Muralistas' intentional use of culturally affirming everyday representations of Chicanas/os and Latinas/os led to the development of a warm working relationship between the artists and the public. Rodríguez recalls that one time "some women brought us food—enchiladas, tamales, pupusas, freshly baked bread—and the men brought us beer. [Laughs] It all worked out to be a great meal that day."[43] The sheer spectacle of mural painting, when combined with the artists' use of contemporary and accessible representations, invited ongoing interaction between themselves and their audiences. Alan Barnett, a mural historian, describes how muralists serve as catalysts for social change:

> The impulse to create a visual environment is the artist's way of trying by the means he has at his control to change the character of daily life. Most muralists know that painting is not enough, but the more people become involved in the actual painting or talking about it, change begins to occur.[44]

Frequently, as they painted, Mujeres Muralistas artists would receive suggestions and recommendations from people on the street. Hernández speaks to the mixed blessings that resulted from the public nature of mural work:

> When you go out on the street, everybody comes around. . . . [I]t can be a drag when you have the winos and druggies coming around trying to rip you off, . . . and it can be really interesting in terms of finding out what people think or how they perceived the work. When we started painting all these images of people from different places in Latin America, we provided a new way of looking at things. It was sort of an urban, multicultural view. [Since] we were painting images that people responded to, they felt like they could come up to us and say things like "Where's the mulattos?" or "I'm from Venezuela and we're not up there."[45]

Mujeres Muralistas' representations in *Latinoamerica* fused the various cultures found in the Mission and provided an artistic statement about the possible connections among Latina/o ethnic groups. Barnett describes murals with such representational characteristics as heritage murals. He notes that their significance lies in their ability to inform and motivate the public to collective action. Barnett specifically describes *Latinoamerica* as a heritage mural:

> Heritage murals[,] . . . by reminding people of the uniqueness of their way of life, and the achievements of the past, stimulated energy for organizing . . . in San Francisco's Mission District where the majority of people derive from different Latin American countries—some urban, others from rural backgrounds. . . . [The mural *Latinoamerica*] has special relevance because the image of the family was shared and affirmed a common Raza.[46]

Mesa-Bains provides insightful commentary on *Latinoamerica* by situating her critique at the intersection of ritual, collective memory, storytelling, and the quotidian:

> The images of their murals *Latinoamerica* and *Paco's Tacos* [*Para el Mercado*], expressed a Pan-American aesthetic where highly visible images of women and emphasis on ceremony, celebration, caretaking, harvest, and a continental terrain worked toward the creation of a new mythology. The power of the murals relied on precisely that widely held memory of the everyday which allowed the work of the Mujeres Muralistas to provide a recollective function for a broad community.[47]

Looking back on that mural, Rodríguez describes the groundbreaking multiethnic consciousness it represents:

> It was one of the first murals in this country to capture what we are like in the U.S. It was an important step, a historical turning point because it [the iconography of the mural] contained a lot of history, but we projected it in a different way. We focused on the people who live here. Who we are and where we came from.[48]

By choosing to portray a range of Latin American cultures, Mexican, Peruvian, Venezuelan, Bolivian, Guatemalan, indigenous, mestiza/o, rural, and urban, in the mural *Latinoamerica,* the artists provided themselves with a representational means for cohering their individualized approaches to mural painting. As a result, the eclectic style of their art underscored the theme of Latina/o heterogeneity. The way in which they organized the design element of color served to connect the various components of the mural and balance their differentiated styles. These matters, in addition to the fact that this mural provided the space for the group to emerge, point to the need for a close reading of its visual representations.

Latinoamerica: Representations of the Quotidian and Diasporic Imagery

As the eye moves from left to right and from top to bottom, the mural's design operates within two vertical and two horizontal planes. Each of the four sections has an upper and a lower focal point. The two vertical sections of the mural serve as visual bookends and ground the horizontal movement of the interior scenes. Beginning with the uppermost left corner, there is an orange and red crescent moon painted with a face. Hanging next to the moon is a bright yellow star; both celestial bodies float in a dark blue expanse. In the opposing upper right corner, a sun, also with an orange and red painted face, hangs in a light blue field of color.

Returning to the left side of the mural, below the crescent moon are four brown, black, and white llamas, three adults and a baby. The adult llamas are carrying packs as though going to market, and all are looking onto a Peruvian pastoral scene. Three male and two female figures are situated in a semicircle, as though in a ritual or dance. The men are playing pipes and the women are bearing backpacks, and one of the women is carrying an infant in her pack. The figures are involved in their own world and detached from the scene above them, a male figure that is weaving a reed boat along the shore of a lake. In the background is a skyline of mountains that forms a perimeter around the lake; through the use of color, the painting incorporates and masks the forward jut of a security light by including it in the mountain range.

Beneath the Peruvian scenes is painted a stone wall, which separates those images from the figures in the lower left-hand corner. Two saguaro cacti stand next to a tree of life, in front of which stand two women dressed in indigenous garb. The women serenely observe the scenes that span the remaining three quarters of the mural space. Below the women is one of twelve cacti, magueyes, which frame and ground the full length of the mural's bottom edge.

Interspersed between the cacti are vertical stalks of maize, growing from rows that emerge from three horizontal planes that ascend from the bottom edge of the mural to its mid-horizon point. The maize functions as a framing device for the different scenes that are taking place within the horizontal planes above them; the rows of maize are growing from earth that has been plowed into rows; the rows serve to bring a perspective to the work that moves the viewer's eye from top to bottom and from left to right and right to left, into the center of the mural.

The left center portion of the mural, framed by two palm trees that emerge from the rows of the maize, contains a quartet of dancing figures dressed in indigenous Venezuelan costume, complete with devil masks. The right center portion of the mural contains a Bolivian devil dancer who faces out toward the audience; regardless of the angle, the eyes on the mask of the Bolivian dancer always seem to be looking directly at the viewer. Both of the dancer's hands are thrown up and out over her head. Her right hand cuts into the rays emanating from the zia, a Navajo sun/star symbol, situated in the direct center of the mural. Another Navajo symbol, the roadrunner, stands below the zia looking up into the scene within the sun/star.

The interior of the zia contains two contemporary, urban adult figures. Their gender is indeterminate, but it is clear from their features that they are of African descent. Four children are held in the circle of one adult's arms, and the other adult holds a blue bird in her hand. The circumference of the zia can barely contain all the human figures within; however, it is not the humans but the zia's brilliant yellow rays that explode out of the confining space and onto the open horizontal plane. Behind the zia, the sky's color changes from dark to light blue, and below it is a valley, whose furrowed earth is framed by a mountain cascade. Two braying burros, without burden or pack, emerge from the valley.

Immediately below this valley scene is a painted frieze that contains a partially concealed Aztec icon. The head of a contemporary woman, a Latina of African descent, holding a teenage girl and standing next to a man, obscures the mask. They are surrounded by contemporary San Francisco scenes, of Mission Street and of a schoolroom, painted in black and white. These figures contrast sharply against the other portions of the mural that are painted in bright vivid colors. Their modern, urban clothing distinguishes them from the predominantly rural, indigenous representations found elsewhere in the mural.

This final section is composed of two groups of people, surrounded by palm trees that span the distance from the bottom to the top of the mural. The uppermost human figures are two indigenous Guatemalan women, carrying pots, household utensils, and an infant. Four parrots surround them; a fifth parrot sits on the shoulder of one of the women. Like the parrots, the women are perched on the limbs of a coffee plant. The branches of the tree shelter a Mayan woman and man, each standing next to a child. The woman is framed by an arabesque geometric design, and the man stands in front of a Mayan glyph; two more parrots that are perched in the surrounding coffee trees observe this scene.

There are three themes that weave together the mural's representations: the family, fecundity and regeneration, and agrarian labor. There are four other motifs whose transgressive quality is important to note: the participatory social role of women, the androgyny of some of the figures, the muted representation of lesbians, and a differentiated rendering of mestizaje. I call these motifs transgressive because at the time the mural was painted, in 1974, some of the subjects represented in the mural were not yet a part of public discourse, either in the manner or with the consciousness in which they are discussed today. I begin by discussing these transgressive themes.

First, women play a central role throughout the mural. Of the thirty-four human figures contained in the mural, twelve are representations of adult women, six are representations of adult men, seven are adults whose gender cannot be determined, two are infants, and seven are children. Second, although the androgynous quality of the seven adult figures was not intentional,[49] and is perhaps a product of the viewer coming to the mural with a transgendered optic, the representations exist nonetheless. For instance, a visual reading of the adult figure in the foreground of the scene contained within the zia shows her/his arms emerging from rolled-up shirtsleeves and her/his hair short-cropped. These are the only body parts visible to the viewer, and she/he is visually distinguished from the adult figure in the background, who in addition to wearing long hair and embracing the children in a classic pose of mothering, has been given cleavage that is visible through her/his T-shirt.

Third, although there was no attempt to create images of lesbians, the artists did paint representations that for them signaled "the undercurrent of rebellion within us by painting figures of women a little too close together."[50] Examples of this type of muted representation can be seen in the two indigenous Mexican women in the upper left-hand corner and the two Guatemalan women in the upper right-hand corner. Hernández described the muralistas as being mindful of the fact that although they might have wanted to be more overt in their representations, "it doesn't happen, especially when somebody else is paying for [the painting of the mural], and especially if it's not necessarily an appropriate setting."[51]

Fourth, the representations in this mural are notable for breaking away from the rendering of mestizaje as an India/o-Spanish mixing of culture. In this work mestizaje is portrayed through the use of Latinas of African descent. The central figures of the only two contemporary urban scenes are clearly of African descent, with their dark skin, nappy hair, broad noses, and lush-lipped mouths. The artists wished to show the range of Latina/o culture, but their intention was not so large as the reconfiguration of the representational paradigm of mestizaje.[52] However, given that the overall representational claim of the mural is its depiction of *Latinoamerica,* it seems appropriate to conclude that the artists' transgressive iconography effected some public thought and discussion within the Mission District's Latina/o community.

One notes that the familial settings, which display tender interactions between mother and child/ren, are those depicting the Latinas/os of African descent. The eyes of each of these figures point out of the frame of the mural directly toward the viewer. Simultaneously, the tight embrace with which the mothers encircle their children is evident. The mother figure contained in the zia has a well-developed, muscular arm that protects the children from the outside; the other contemporary mother figure similarly guards her girl child using both of her arms.

As though to underscore the importance of the family, three protective Venezuelan devil figures dance while looking onto the family scene in the zia. A fourth devil figure kneels before the family in homage and appears to be giving the group his blessing of safekeeping. These figures are not threatening but rather are intended to ward off the evils that might befall the family. The largest figure in the mural is that of the Bolivian devil dancer, who fills almost three quarters of the panel's twenty-foot-high expanse as she stands opposed to the Venezuelan devil dancers on the other side of the zia. With outstretched arms flung wide open and her oversized hands—which are almost as large as the mask covering her face—she, too, gives her protective benediction. The eyes on the mask of the Bolivian devil dancer follow the viewer regardless of where one is standing. It is as though the dancer is able to protect the mural itself from harm outside of its frame.

The artists' emphasis on fecundity and regeneration is evident in their representational uses of the tree of life, maguey, maize, water, and the earth. The tree of life is, of course, not only confined to Latin American culture in its symbology as the originating source of life on earth. The elements of water and earth, particularly as they are depicted in this mural, as a lake into which a fisherman will take his soon-to-be-completed reed boat and as furrowed and planted plains of land, stand as emblems of the renewable use of natural resources. The use of the maguey plant and maize as signs of fecundity and regeneration is particular to Latin America. For people of Mexican and Central American descent, the corn plant is the living manifestation of the cyclical process of regeneration, and proof that the life force never dies.[53] The maguey plant, from which many life-benefiting products come—the potent ritual-related drink pulque, fibers for weaving cloth and making rope, thorns for needles, and leaves for paper making, roofing, and food—is also linked to the processes of regeneration. The plant's prolific reproductive quality is often metaphorically connected to female fecundity.[54]

As though to emphasize to the cyclical nature of life working through the regenerative process, an Aztec mask of the goddess Tlaltecuhtli is found within the space of the painted frieze, located immediately below the left hand of the Bolivian devil dancer. She is the Aztec Earth Monster from whom all life comes. Tlaltecuhtli, with her open-jawed, toothsome face, is sometimes depicted in a childbearing squatting position, although that is not the case in this mural. Her open mouth is the passage to the under-world, located inside of the earth. Thus she represents both life and death. She generates life and all living things but also takes them back into herself.[55] In addition to these regenerative, agrarian signs, the artists made connections to the labor involved in fishing, farming, and the marketing of handmade goods. The Guatemalan women are bearing pots and utensils and the llamas are carrying full packs as though going to (or coming from) market.

Latinoamerica stands as an excellent example of how the quotidian has been brought forth into the development of a Chicana aesthetic expression without succumbing to the pressures of popular imagery or traditional historiography. The artists of Mujeres Muralistas incorporated a variety of representations from different Latina/o cultures and from different historical moments, such as the use of Tlaltecuhtli juxtaposed to the images of contemporary urban families. Although their work might be characterized as celebratory rather than a critique of Latina/o cultures, they balanced their affirmative impulse with the acknowledgment of social difficulties. This acknowledgment is seen in the representations of the devil dancers that protect the various families. Although labor is not the central activity of the mural, the role of work in the lives of the people depicted is not too far from the rituals and moments in which they are engaged; women are bearing goods, a fisherman repairs his boat, llamas stand ready for market, and the burros await their packs.

By weaving the daily elements of Latina/o life with the expressly twentieth-century detail of their imagery, the artists of Mujeres Muralistas marked with this mural a unique moment in the development of the Chicano Art Movement. The mural was dedicated on May 31, 1974, and as is the tradition in community mural artwork, it was presented to the community with a grand celebration. The festivities included the core artists and assistants of Mujeres Muralistas, civic dignitaries, officials of the Model Cities Program, and, of course, the many Mission District Latina/o residents who served as the inspiration for the representations in *Latinoamerica*.[56] Some years later, when the Model Cities Program was terminated, the building was sold and regrettably the new owner had the mural painted over. This might not happen today, when zoning laws and state copyright laws offer protection to muralists and their art.[57] Although *Latinoamerica* is no longer available to the general public on a daily basis, its groundbreaking visual representations of Latina/o families, the role of women, labor, and the construction of mestizaje hold significant social and cultural lessons that still resonate in the twenty-first century.

Evolution of a Legacy

Mujeres Muralistas continued their thematic portrayals of the quotidian in their three subsequent murals. Immediately after completing *Latinoamerica*, they were asked to paint another work. The owner of Paco's Tacos located then at South Van Ness and Twenty-fourth Streets commissioned *Para el Mercado*. The owner, as well as many Mission District residents, opposed the planned construction of a McDonald's drive-in. They saw it as an inappropriate intrusion by Big Business into what was then the mom-and-pop character of commerce in the Mission. The owner asked the muralists to paint something that would impart the importance of eating fresh, locally grown food from neighborhood markets and that would evoke the marketplace that all Latinas/os recall from their native lands or from rural regions in the United States.

Carrillo and Méndez were the core artists for this work.[58] The wall for the mural ran the length of the parking lot alongside the *taquería,* and the two artists divided the space in half with each taking a side. The artistic styles are quite distinct, and once again color and subject matter were used to organize the mural. Méndez's portion of the wall shows people, men and women, fishing and harvesting crops. Carrillo's section is of the marketplace where adults and children are selling, admiring, and purchasing the many wares available, including pineapples, wild birds, and baskets. The mural was dedicated with a celebration on September 15, 1974. The wall has since been razed, but legend has it that a portion was stolen and another portion salvaged and stored nearby at the Precita Eyes Mural Arts Center.[59]

Their next work, *Rhomboidal Parallelogram,* was a freestanding, three-dimensional mural commissioned by the San Francisco Art Commission and exhibited at the 1975 San Francisco Art Festival. Méndez, Pérez, and Rodríguez accepted the commission, and Hernández joined in later. Pérez recalled the unusual format: "We decided to do something totally different, because they had no walls for us to paint on. We decided to do a three-dimensional geometrical mural."[61] A six-paneled painting-construction, on completion it was ten feet high and thirteen feet long. The mural's unconventional format allowed the artists to continue their usual operating method of dividing the mural into sections, with each artist designing her section. Pérez recalls:

> Each one of us took a panel. We decided to paint scenes of women doing different things, some traditional and some nontraditional. Like I painted this curandera with a chola. Ester did one panel with a farmworker. Consuelo painted a factory worker.[61]

It is thought that this mural is stored in a warehouse owned by the Art Commission. However, it is unclear if this is indeed the case. Because the commission paid for the work, on completion the artwork became its property. The government entity took possession of the mural after the closing of the exhibition for which it was painted. Méndez left the group at this time, citing her desire to create more political art: "I was really enjoying the opportunities to work in the community. But I felt as though it was important to portray images that were less cultural and more political. There were important stories and lessons to be told, and we weren't doing it."[62]

Méndez's departure was accompanied by an internal debate over matters such as determining who was a core artist as opposed to an assistant or the fact that the group's members were split on whether to admit an Angla muralist, Susan Kelk Cervantes, as a member. Any one of these issues would have been difficult to resolve in any group, let alone one in which internal organization and systems were never priorities. These factors added to the already complex creative situation of disparate artists working within a cooperative setting, with limited resources and differing levels of time and interest.

It was in this environment in 1975 that the fourth and final Mujeres Muralistas project, *Fantasy World for Children,* was painted in Mini-Park, located one block from La Galería de la Raza. The coordinating artists were Pérez, Carrillo, and Rodríguez. Mini-Park was a small playground surrounded by the walls of the neighboring homes. This is the only existing mural work painted predominantly by members of the originating group.[63] Pérez, Carrillo, and Rodríguez convened for what would be the final mural ascribed to a majority of the originating artists of Mujeres Muralistas. Their works on Balmy Alley were phantasmal, as are the renderings at Mini-Park. The park mural draws from the fantastical as the artists visually blended the varied ecological terrain of Latin America. Lush green fronds evoke a rainforest landscape, while an active volcano belches a psychedelic plume into the brilliant blue sky. The artists created a magical topography where brown-skinned children explore while smiling jaguars and dinosaurs walk among snakes, flamingos, sea turtles, peacocks, and quetzals.

Other artists would take up the legacy of Mujeres Muralistas and honor their work by continuing the name of the collective. However, the eloquence and force of the artistry of the originating members, particularly in *Latinoamerica,* remains unique. The artwork of Mujeres Muralistas was an important contribution to the development of the Chicano Art Movement. Not only did this group of mujeres assemble themselves in defiance of conventional opinion, but they also created challenging and innovative representations in the spirit of a collective endeavor without giving over their individual styles. Further, they provided in their murals critical and foundational representations of Latina/o diasporic imagery. That each of these artists continues to be prodigious in her creative works and remains involved in the current wave of the Chicano Art Movement speaks to their individual commitment and also to the strength of their creative influence.

Notes

1. Victoria Quintero, "A Mural Is a Painting on a Wall Done by Human Hands," *El Tecolote* 5, no. 1 (1974).
2. Sybil Venegas, "The Artists and Their Work—The Social Role of the Chicana Artist," *ChisméArte* 1, no. 4 (1977); Alan W. Barnett, *Community Murals: The People's Art* (New York: Art Alliance Press, 1984); Shifra Goldman, "How, Why, Where, and When It All Happened: Chicano Murals of California," and Amalia Mesa-Bains, "Quest for Identity: Profile of Two Chicana Muralists based on Interviews with Judith F. Baca and Patricia Rodríguez," in *Signs from the Heart: California Chicano Murals,* ed. Eva Sperling Cockcroft and Holly Barnet-Sánchez (Albuquerque: University of New Mexico Press, 1990); Amalia Mesa-Bains, "El Mundo Feminino: Chicana Artists of the Movement—A Commentary on Development and Production," in *CARA: Chicano Art: Resistance and Affirmation, 1965–1985* (Los Angeles: Wight Art Gallery–UCLA, 1991); Timothy W. Drescher, *San Francisco Murals: Community Creates Its Muse, 1914-1994,* 2d ed. (St. Paul: Pogo Press, 1994); Shifra Goldman, "Portraying Ourselves: Contemporary Chicana Artists" and "Mujeres de California: Latin American Women Artists," in *Dimensions of the Americas: Art and Social Change in Latin America and the United States,* by Shifra M. Goldman (Chicago: University of Chicago Press, 1994); Eva Cockcroft, John Pitman Weber, and James Cockcroft, *Toward a People's Art: The Contemporary Mural Movement,* 2d ed. (Albuquerque: University of New Mexico Press, 1998).
3. Drescher, *San Francisco Murals,* 14.
4. See Eve Cockcroft, "Women in the Community Mural Movement," *Community Murals Magazine* (1976); Quintero, "A Mural Is a Painting."
5. Ester Hernández, interview, September 17, 1993.
6. Irene Pérez, interview, September 20, 1993; Consuelo Méndez, interview, November 13, 1994; Patricia Rodríguez, interview, October 21, 1999.
7. Consuelo Méndez, interview, November 13, 1994.
8. Irene Pérez, interview, September 20, 1993.
9. Patricia Rodríguez, interview, October 21, 1999.
10. Chela Sandoval, *Methodology of the Oppressed,* Theory Out of Bounds series (Minneapolis: University of Minnesota, 2000), 62.
11. Audre Lorde, "The Master's Tools Will Never Dismantle the Master's House," in *This Bridge Called My Back: Writings by Radical Women of Color,* ed. Cherríe Moraga and Gloria Anzaldúa, 2d ed. (New York: Kitchen Table: Women of Color Press, 1983), 99.
12. I borrow from Amalia Mesa-Bains when I refer to "altar-installations." She applies the category to distinguish the public art form from the more intimate, sacred space of the domestic altar.

13. Tomás Ybarra-Frausto, "Recuerdo, Descubrimiento, Voluntad: Mexican/Chicano Customs for Day of the Dead," in *Día de Los Muertos* (Chicago: Mexican Fine Arts Center Museum, 1991), 24–30.

14. The annual Día de Los Muertos exhibitions are held variously at La Galería de la Raza, the Mission Cultural Center, and La Raza Graphics Center in San Francisco where installations include those created in memory of people who have died from AIDS, Lebanese and Palestinian war victims, and farmworkers dead from pesticide exposure. In the area of mural art, the Oakland–San Francisco Bay Area has a long history of collaboration among different ethnic and cultural groups. In 1993 the San Francisco Women's Building commissioned *Maestrapeace,* a work whose artistic splendor and representational complexity stands unparalleled in the history of Bay Area murals. The core artists included Juana Alicia, Miranda Bergman, Edythe Boone, Susan Kelk Cervantes, Meera Desai, Yvonne Littleton, and Irene Pérez.

15. Drescher, *San Francisco Murals,* 7.

16. *Mission Mural Walk* map (San Francisco: Precita Eyes Mural Arts Center, 1993).

17. Irene Pérez, interview, September 20, 1993.

18. Drescher, *San Francisco Murals,* 90–92.

19. Irene Pérez, interview, September 20, 1993.

20. According to Hernández, she was asked by the Chávez family to create a graphic of César Chávez that was subsequently submitted to the U.S. Postal Service as the union and the family's petition for a stamp commemorating the labor leader's work. Ester Hernández, interview, September 17, 1993. Hers was not the image selected.

21. Venegas, "The Artists and Their Work," 3.

22. Malaquías Montoya, interview, October 4, 1994.

23. Irene Pérez, interview, September 20, 1993. Assistants included Ester Hernández, Miriam Olivo, Ruth Rodríguez, and Susan Kelk Cervantes.

24. Consuelo Méndez, interview, November 13, 1994.

25. Patricia Rodríguez, interview, October 21, 1999.

26. Irene Pérez, interview, September 20, 1993.

27. Ibid.

28. Ibid.

29. Patricia Rodríguez, interview, October 21, 1999.

30. Ibid.

31. Patricia Kerr, "Las Mujeres Muralistas," in *Connecting Conversations: Interviews with 28 Bay Area Women Artists,* ed. Moira Roth (Oakland: Eucalyptus Press, 1988), 133.

32. Irene Pérez, interview, September 20, 1993.

33. Patricia Rodríguez, interview, October 21, 1999.

34. Goldman, *Dimensions of the Americas,* 213. The other interview is found in Kerr, "Las Mujeres Muralistas," 131–36.

35. Ester Hernández, interview, September 17, 1993.

36. Mesa-Bains, "El Mundo Feminino," 138.

37. Irene Pérez, interview, September 20, 1993.

38. Ester Hernández, interview, September 17, 1993.

39. Ibid.

40. Irene Pérez, interview, September 20, 1993.

41. Ester Hernández, interview, September 17, 1993.

42. Drescher, *San Francisco Murals,* 22.

43. Patricia Rodríguez, interview, October 21, 1999.
44. Barnett, *Community Murals,* 134.
45. Ester Hernández, interview, September 17, 1993.
46. Barnett, *Community Murals,* 136.
47. Mesa-Bains, "Quest for Identity," 76.
48. Kerr, "Las Mujeres Muralistas," 134.
49. Irene Pérez, interview, September 20, 1993.
50. Ester Hernández, interview, September 17, 1993.
51. Ibid.
52. Ibid.
53. Roberta H. Markham and Peter T. Markham, *The Flayed God: The Mesoamerican Mythological Tradition: Sacred Texts and Images from Pre-Columbian Mexico and Central America* (San Francisco: Harper–San Francisco, 1992), 182.
54. Ibid., 185.
55. Ibid., 227.
56. Irene Pérez, interview, September 20, 1993.
57. There have been numerous incidents in which murals with historical significance were painted over by owners claiming ignorance of the law.
58. They received assistance from Susan Kelk Cervantes and Miriam Olivo. Drescher, *San Francisco Murals,* 90.
59. Timothy W. Drescher, personal communication, June 25, 2002.
60. Irene Pérez, interview, September 20, 1993.
61. Ibid.
62. Consuelo Méndez, interview, November 13, 1994.
63. Irene Pérez, interview, September 20, 1993.

THREE

Co-Madres Artistas

"We Belong to the Community"

Chance and circumstance were the progenitors of the Chicana artists collective Co-Madres Artistas. During winter 1992, the coordinator of a conference on Latina leadership decided to include an exhibition of artwork by Chicanas in the program. While researching Sacramento-based Chicana artists, the organizer was directed to Irma Lerma Barbosa. Barbosa contacted six other artists and invited them to participate in the exhibition.[1] The two-day exhibition received critical acclaim, and its success generated the collective. From that moment to the present, Co-Madres Artistas has produced art for exhibition. Their mutual support is deep and abiding. Between 1992 and 2002, the collective was featured in more than fifty-three exhibitions.[2] Members whose interviews are included in this volume are Barbosa, Carmel Castillo, Laura Llano, Mareia de Socorro, and Helen Villa. Lucy Montoya Rhodes served as the collective's administrator and was also interviewed for this project.

Easel painting is the dominant form of the Co-Madres Artistas members, who use a variety of techniques and materials. Barbosa works in oils, pastel, and acrylic. Castillo works in pastel, charcoal, acrylic, and oils. Llano paints only in watercolor, a technique she describes as "dangerous, unpredictable, unforgiving, and magical."[3] Villa paints primarily in acrylic, and Socorro works in acrylic, charcoal, graphite, oils, pastel, and watercolor. Socorro began to paint with oils thirty years before her work with Co-Madres Artistas but left that medium because, she said, she had "no time to wait for it to dry."[4]

Co-Madres Artistas are responsible for selecting the works that are displayed in their exhibitions, as well as for the installation of their work. They are also involved in public relations efforts connected to their exhibitions. The collective defies neat categorization. Each of the members attended college, and most have acquired advanced degrees. Three of the five artists interviewed have had entrepreneurial experience in the visual arts. All the artists work outside of the home to support their families, place a high value on their families, and balance their careers with other interests.[5]

Their employment and family responsibilities left them with little time or energy to pursue their own artwork with any consistency or intensity. Some of the artists owned art-related businesses, which helped to satisfy both their creative impulses and their need for income. Some members found other ways, such as teaching art in the public schools, to combine their commitment to art and their need to work. During the years before Co-Madres Artistas was formed, the artists enrolled in art classes to further develop their techniques.

Most of the artists knew each other before the collective was established, and in some cases their relationships had spanned more than thirty years. Many of these friendships grew out of their involvement in the cultural institutions that are central to the Sacramento Valley Chicana/o community, such as the Royal Chicano Air Force, begun in 1969, and Galería Posada, founded in 1972.[6] Over the years, the La Raza artists who would later form Co-Madres Artistas encountered each other at RCAF or La Raza Galería Posada events. Helen Villa recalls:

> I used to see Irma and Laura at different cultural events[,] . . . usually art shows that the RCAF artists were putting on. We would always say, "Hi! Are you painting? Are you doing any art?" We would always respond, "Well, I haven't had a chance to, . . . the kids and everything." One day, Irma said, "This is it. We have a chance to exhibit, get your stuff out."[7]

Barbosa describes the process that led to the birth of the group:

> I was going to show my work in this show, right? But then I thought, Damn, I feel really alone. So I went to a friend . . . and said, "I'm going to have this opportunity, and I think it would be a good idea if I invited other Chicana artists to exhibit."[8]

Until Barbosa's call to exhibit, Carmel Castillo had painted irregularly. The 1982 death of her husband, the renowned Chicano artist Carlos Licón, had left her with little creative energy, and she filled her time primarily by working vigorously as chair of the membership committee of La Raza Galería Posada. The invitation to participate in the exhibition gave her the opportunity to return to her painting. As she recalls, "I [had] put my [art]work aside, until Irma contacted me. Then I resumed painting again, and I've done a lot more than I had in many, many years."[9]

Laura Llano met Barbosa in college during the 1970s and just before Barbosa's invitation began painting after a ten-year hiatus. She recounts the changes in her personal life that precipitated her return to painting:

> In 1990 I was in the middle of a divorce and my daughter was at an age where I knew it was going to be hard on her. But once I made the decision, I said to myself, I just have to live through it. But, what am I going to do now? After ten years of not painting, I said, OK, it's time to do some art! It was during the summertime, and every day I got up and kept to my promise. I'd go for a walk[,] . . . come back, shower, and I would paint or draw or do something with my art.[10]

Lucy Montoya Rhodes, administrator of the first exhibition, had recently experienced difficulties in her personal life. Her husband had died quite suddenly, and she was left a single parent. Barbosa was responsible for inviting Montoya Rhodes into the organization. She remembers:

> I met Lucy Montoya in 1969 at a local meeting for the Brown Beret organization of Sacramento. We were roommates for a while. As time passed, we each married and had children. We reconnected when Lucy contacted me around 1992. We were both having some personal difficulties. Her husband had died in a tragic diving accident and I was going through a divorce. I called upon Lucy when the Co-Madres organization formed. Lucy is the most loving and unselfish woman friend I have ever had the benefit of knowing and loving. She embodies all of the very best qualities of the ideal Co-Madre. I trust her with my children and my heart.[11]

Participation in Co-Madres Artistas gave Montoya Rhodes a sense of community and the opportunity for social involvement, and the group benefited from her administrative skills. She describes her contributions in this way:

> You know, because I'm not an artist I come at this differently than the others. I can see things they don't see. Plus, I like to keep things organized. I keep things going. It can be difficult at times, you know, . . . telling people what they are supposed to be doing. But they listen to me, [laughs] mostly![12]

Although Mareia de Socorro was present for the initial planning meeting, she did not exhibit her work in the first show. At that time, she had undergone surgery on both hands and one arm was in a cast, so she was unable to paint.[13]

Co-Madres Artistas is a resourceful, self-reliant group. The majority of money for supplies, travel, and marketing comes from the individual artists with some support from family and friends. Co-Madres Artistas members applied to the California Arts Council (CAC) 1993 Multicultural Entry Grants program for funding to underwrite the costs of their outreach and publicity activities. Because the artists produce works primarily for exhibition, these activities are crucial to their success.

Co-Madres Artistas received $2,000 for 1993–94. This was a matching grant whose terms stipulated that for every dollar the CAC gave Co-Madres Artistas, the group was expected to raise fifty cents. The grant carried with it the possibility of refunding at the same level for up to two additional years. The availability of the multiyear grant was predicated on the success with which the group met its fiscal and activity goals for the previous year. In the first grant cycle, Co-Madres Artistas used the funds to create and exhibit art, including the purchase of art and framing supplies and the duplication and mailing of an introduction packet.[14] The packet contained a cover letter, a brochure, artists' biographies, and copies of published reviews. These materials were mailed to art-related businesses, museums, and galleries. Villa wrote to the California Arts Council to report on their progress:

> Our production of art has increased, and invitations to exhibit are growing. Our recognition and respect in the art community has increased. Media coverage through interviews, reviews, and articles on our group has been positive. In addition, our experience working with galleries and art centers has broadened. We have been

more productive in our artwork because of exhibit deadlines. We have each improved in the development of our art styles and have upcoming opportunities to experience different media.[15]

Story/Visions from the Cactus Tree

The publication of *Story/Visions from the Cactus Tree: A Catalogue of Fine Art*[16] was key to Co-Madres Artistas' marketing and outreach strategies in the mid-1990s. The catalog's initial circulation reached approximately three hundred northern California visual arts organizations, including venues large and small, obscure and well known. The way in which Co-Madres Artistas presented their catalog reflects their dual allegiance to highly personalized art and to commercial endeavors. The twenty-page, glossy publication contains a full-color and a black-and-white reproduction of two artworks by each Co-Madres Artistas member.

The publication of the catalog was more than a year in the making and was a milestone in the development of Co-Madres Artistas. This highly talented group of middle-aged, middle-class Chicanas renewed their personal commitment and artistic contributions as cultural workers. Their emergence as mature artists came after a decades-long hiatus during which they were employed, raised families, and dealt with life's personal triumphs and struggles. The catalog serves as the exhibition site through which I discuss the art and creative processes of Co-Madres Artistas.

Four of the five members of Co-Madres Artistas were entrepreneurs in addition to their full-time jobs. Their backgrounds in business gave the group a commercial character. They created their own logo, developed marketing tools, looked for ways to exhibit their art that would give them the best sales opportunities, and developed a Web site. In describing the group as commercially inclined, I am not saying that the representations they created were commercialized or conceived so as to prompt sales. The artwork of Co-Madres Artistas emerged from their roles as social agents and cultural workers who were interested in presenting their formulations of a Chicana aesthetic. By situating themselves as artists and business-women, the members of Co-Madres Artistas problematized their identities as cultural workers.

Their unwillingness to succumb to easily understood positionalities is most sharply illustrated in the way that the artists retain possession of their original artwork and resist its loss to private collectors. The artists are able to accomplish this control by reproducing their paintings as Cibachrome® photographs, also called C prints. Each artist attempts to have at least a few of her works available in this format. The C prints, usually eight inches by ten inches, are considerably smaller in size than the original paintings, which are as large as five feet by four feet. In many of their exhibitions, original artworks are displayed alongside framed C prints. None of the originals are offered for sale, but there is a price list available for the limited-edition prints.

Their self-produced catalog is a manifestation of the collective's artistic aspirations and commercial sensibilities. Laura Llano created the image for the cover, a tall saguaro cactus that stands in an indeterminate landscape. Three cactus stems grow from a central trunk, and five mandalas surround the cactus. A single stemmed cactus stands in front of the larger one. Each mandala contains a visual signifier representing one of the Co-Madres Artistas. The highest-placed mandala contains the head of a woman, a *curandera*, and behind her is a swirling miasma symbolic of her energy source. The curandera signifies Castillo, who uses the figure in many of her works. Moving clockwise, the next mandala contains two cactus flowers, each of which emerges from two nopal leaves. It is the image that Barbosa chose for herself. The next mandala includes a flowering cactus with a microscopic view of its flower bud; the imagery represents Llano. Next is Socorro's attributive mandala, a fish that lies between two hands as though in offering. Immediately above is Villa's image; it is a mandala that contains a three-sided face, a sign frequently used to represent the ethnic strands that comprise Raza. The mestiza is in the center, and her visage is formed by the blending of the India and Spanish faces that frame it.

Inside the catalog are prefatory remarks by the group, in which they acknowledge the assistance of family and friends and summarize their history as a collective. Retired art professor and founding RCAF member, Esteban Villa, introduces the catalog by framing the collective's art with a description of each artist's style and strengths. Villa's introduction is similar to those found in most exhibition catalogs—in that he provides the audience with a visual and historical context for the works contained within. It is a playfully respectful piece. Because he taught each of the Co-Madres Artistas, he is able to reflect on their development as artists. What we learn in Villa's essay are pieces of personal information about each of the artists, which he purposefully links to their work as artists. He also comments on the groups' external and internal dynamics:

Co-Madres Artistas and the community are synonymous. The contribution to the community by each member adds to the pride of the group. Individualism within the group is encouraged. It's a revelation to see each artist develop her style and aesthetic appeal. It is interesting to note how this Co-Madres organization nurtures the individual's self-confidence and self-esteem to become one with nature.[17]

Theresa Harlan, then curator of the C. N. Gorman Museum at the University of California, Davis, describes in her essay the ways in which Co-Madres Artistas engage in cooperative activities that result in a communality of spirit and art. In particular, she describes the centrality of Chicana identity to their work:

> The significance of Co-Madres Artistas is not just solely located in the idea and notion of a women's art collective, but grounded in years of community service, contribution to the arts, and the resulting messages of art that originate from a Chicana/Latina self-identity, experience, and history.[18]

On the page opposing her essay is a list of the artists' names and addresses and the titles of the paintings reproduced in the catalog. The overall treatment of the narrative and visual material that follows in the main text is the same for each of the artists. Each artist has a two-page spread with a full-page color reproduction, a smaller three-quarter-page black-and-white plate, and her descriptions of the works; the artist's signature brands the bottom portion of the page. Works are displayed in alphabetical order: Castillo, Barbosa, Llano, Villa, and Socorro.[19] The ensuing discussion of Co-Madres Artistas follows the order in which the artists are presented in the publication; each section opens with a brief statement by the artist.

CARMEL CASTILLO

> I believe that art is a pathway to the spirit. In my Mujer images, I see India de la Tierra, Mother Earth, Goddess and Healer, representing harmony among all living things. My metaphysical images revere Mother Earth and the power of female energies. *May the Great Spirit protect you and Mother Earth Bless you.*[20]

Carmel Castillo's late husband, Carlos Licón, influences her work as an artist. Although she was a working artist long before she met her husband in the mid-1960s, his style, subjects, and use of materials are reflected in Castillo's paintings. She works in a variety of media but prefers pastels:

> I did oils many, many years before I met Carlos. After I met him, I literally threw my brushes away. He's the one who turned me on to pastels. If I do oils now, I go down to my son's studio and work there. I don't have good ventilation here. I love oils. You can go wild with oils. They're just so much freer, so much looser. Acrylics dry so fast and [they're] not as rewarding as the pastels.[21]

When Castillo first began her relationship with Co-Madres Artistas, she was criticized for her exclusive use of pastels and encouraged to change to oils, a more "serious" technique. She felt that the criticism was framed as much by the artistic materials preferred by some members as it was emblematic of a generation gap:

> When I first started with Co-Madres I did a lot of pastels. Some of the artists said, "Well, that's a lesser work. Why don't you do oils?" I was much older than those members were and I believe that they felt, Well, that's all she can do.[22]

Castillo works in other media but continues to prefer pastels. She believes that her influence in the group can be seen in the fact that other members of Co-Madres Artistas are now working in pastels, in addition to their primary media.[23] The catalog's color reproduction of Castillo's pastel work La India de la Tierra harkens to the Mother Earth imagery she describes in her opening statement. In this figure, Castillo carries out her commitment to depicting "metaphysical images . . . and the power of female energies." The seated female figure fills the entire frame of the painting, with her head and knees spilling off the margins. She is a fecund figure; her full-breasted, large-hipped, fleshy-thighed body slips forward from the background into an angled plane that moves out from the central horizontal surface of the painting and into the extreme foreground. Her long, sweeping hair adds to the fluid quality of the work, as it pours in streamlike rivulets from her head, down her back and chest. Her hair gives added emphasis to the contours of her body, and the India's hands visually aid the flow of the hair in its descent to her pubic area. Although her name is La India de la Tierra, she could equally be called La India de la Agua, as the composition is so fluid.

With her downcast eyes, La India is totally removed from any interaction with the viewer. Her environment has no time or recognizable setting. Her golden skin makes it possible for the texture of the paper to pop out from beneath the colors of the pastels and provides a sensuous quality to her voluptuous figure. The symmetry of her large brown nipple resonates with the shadow of her bellybutton and the swell formed at the point that her belly and hip meet.

The anonymous, disconnected quality of the figure in *La India de la Tierra* contrasts sharply with Castillo's black-and-white selection, *La Curandera*. In this pastel, the healer faces the audience directly. She dispassionately observes whoever comes before her, even as her eyes follow every movement of her audience. The assertive gaze of *La Curandera* is juxtaposed to the power of the reflective moment of *La India de la Tierra*. The healer's eyes follow the viewer relentlessly. She embodies Castillo's description of the power of female energies as a halo organically emerges from her head. The halo contains a variety of swirling, undefined shapes. Her shoulders are shrouded in a robe with a flowerlike print that alternates from a light background with dark flowers on her left side to a dark background with light flowers on her right. The robe is parted in front with a décolletage, but in spite of its low cut, no sign of the curandera's breasts is visible. She is both sensual and restrained. Licón's influence on Castillo is especially evident in *La India de la Tierra*. She describes it as an homage to an earlier work of Licón's:

> That particular painting [*La India Mas Hermosa*] was one of Licón's paintings that I wanted [to keep] badly. But he needed money and loaned the painting to someone in exchange for $300. He never got the painting back. So I did my rendition of it. However, my India is much softer than his is because for me she represents Mother Earth. That is why I've since changed the title to *Madre Tierra*. I have also painted a six-foot-by-four-foot rendition of the same work [*Madre Tierra*] on silk. That version is going to be exhibited in Beijing at the United Nations' International Women's Conference.[24]

In addition to honoring Licón's powerful style in her works, Castillo draws from many of the traditional cultural icons in Chicana/o visual art. Other works of hers include a number of tributes to Frida Kahlo, as well as several still lifes. Her works are distinct from the other Co-Madres Artistas because of the overt spirituality of her subjects. Her subtle handling of pastel is noteworthy, as is her ability to project the complex duality of a restrained sensuality onto the Chicana figure. Castillo speaks of her use of the ethnic quotidian and religious figuration in her representations:

> If you notice in my work, my people are ethnic, they're Mexican. The symbols I use are Mexican. I want to keep this imagery alive. I want to reveal the curandera as an indigenous woman, of the earth. She represents god as healer, who contains an inner strength and purity. She possesses an inner calm. I hope that the viewer can connect with the magic that I want to share.[25]

IRMA LERMA BARBOSA

> Stories are the spirit threads passed on from generation to genera-tion. They are the means of learning. The stories passed on by our elders were meant to guide and develop morals and values. My art takes you on a pilgrimage to mythical places and tells you stories of innocence, beauty, and pure passion. The universality of the Earth Mother theme is utilized within much of my work to communicate that every individual is responsible for their actions and their words as they affect the earth and all people[,] . . . that each person is a walking story[,] . . . and that we are all connected. *May the Great Spirit protect you and Mother Earth Bless you.*[26]

Irma Lerma Barbosa's paintings *Warriors of the New Day* and *Chiapas Madonna* are portraits that emerge from her series of solitary female figures. Barbosa herself was the lone Chicana artist who worked with the Royal Chicano Air Force, although other women were affiliated with the RCAF in other capacities. Barbosa felt that when she worked as an artist in the RCAF her art and personal life were under constant scrutiny. Her role as the sole female artist in an all-male group was the subject of speculation by women and men alike:

> At the start women that were associated with the RCAF never painted. They were enabling within the community by trying to help with grants and funding and holding down jobs. But as much as we

were all working hard, those women didn't trust me. They thought I was some kind of tramp because I worked as an artist, side by side with the men. So I knew I had to handle myself a certain way in order to get their respect. So I'd be sitting around in my combat boots, while the girlfriends would be flittering around the men like butterflies.[27]

There were two defining moments in which Barbosa felt the injurious results of having followed an independent route as a Chicana artist working in the all-male enclave of the RCAF. One had to do with criticism she received regarding the authenticity of her work as Chicano art. Barbosa had studied under the direction of the master artist Tarmo Pasto when he was a professor at Sacramento State College. It was from him that she received a foundation in conventional fine arts. She learned how to stretch canvas onto a frame, take care of her brushes, and employ traditional design elements in the composition of her paintings. In contrast, she believes, the men came to their work from the perspective of graphic artists and cared little for the subtleties Barbosa displayed in her work. They preferred instead to use bold designs and colors. Barbosa describes the criticism she received from one of the RCAF artists:

I was told that I needed to distance myself from Tarmo Pasto because my paintings were "too soft, too pastel," that they weren't vibrant "like the Aztecs." My work was not considered substantial. It was recognized that I was getting my art training from somewhere else, and it wasn't perceived in the most positive way. But it was my choice.[28]

The second incident had to do with the RCAF's tradition of incorporating military language and dress in their public appearances and conferring rank on the members, except for Barbosa.[29] She explains:

One night we were hanging out, sitting around a bonfire. The guys were drinking, and everyone was kickback. José says, "Well, tonight's the night we're going to give Irma her general's wings." One of the guys objected. He said, "No, this is not right. She's a woman. . . ." Blah, blah, blah, he went on. This member was famous for having fits, throwing tantrums. So nobody wanted to make him mad because he would hold a grudge, and then he wouldn't help on the next project. I didn't get my rank as a general. I was hurt and pissed, you know? José told me I would have to become a general of women.[30]

The way in which Barbosa handled the criticism and rejection was to intensify her study with Pasto and to become even more strongly committed to developing her own artistic approach:

I was studying with a world-renowned artist, and that meant I already had a foot in the door. So I just went through the door that Pasto had opened for me. Then I didn't worry about being a foot-soldier. I made myself a general, and I didn't need to announce it. I just lived it by bringing along other women who had creative abilities and leadership qualities.[31]

Thirty years later, Barbosa's commitment to other Chicana artists still stands. Perhaps her commitment is most clearly seen in the way in which she shared the invitation to exhibit that allowed for the artists of Co-Madres Artistas to come together. She also has a tendency in her figurative work to depict women of mythic proportions or to paint stark, challenging settings. Barbosa's oil painting *Warriors of the New Day* was the piece she selected for full-color reproduction in the catalog. It is daybreak, as the title tells us, and there is a woman standing with arms crossed over her abdomen. She is simply but elegantly dressed, in an off-the-shoulder blouse, a skirt with a border of lace, and fashionable sandals. She has wide bracelets on each wrist. One wonders how she comes to be in this remote desert setting. Alone with her thoughts, she seems not at all concerned that her surroundings are simultaneously beautiful and menacing. The central object in the painting is a saguaro cactus covered with hair-like spines, and at its peak there is a blossom. A hummingbird hovers near the blossom. Another cactus is in silhouette to its left and is tipped to one side, almost in the process of falling over; smaller cacti, with many sharp, glowing spines, border the base of the central plant. The ground beneath the cacti is formed of large chunks of soil. This painting may be read as a powerful call for unity between Chicanas and Chicanos. Roberta Markham and Peter Markham, cultural scholars of Mesoamerican traditions, recount an Aztec narrative integral to understanding how this painting evokes reconciliation:

An Aztec migration myth holds the male warrior god, Huitzilopochtli, abandoned his sister, Malinalxoch. This legendary separation coincides with the historical separation of the Mexica Aztecs, the people of Huitzilopochtli, from another group of Aztecs, the people who settled at Malinalco, whose tutelary deity was Malinalxoch. . . . [In the telling of this story] male-female opposition is stressed. . . . [The eventual reunification] must be seen metaphorically as a unity of spirit[,] . . . and both suggest the identity of the Aztec nature with the Aztec destiny.[32]

Barbosa responds to her early experiences as a Chicana artist operating in the largely male field of the Chicano Art Movement not in a retaliatory spirit but in the spirit of rapprochement. She paints the hummingbird, symbol of the male Aztec warrior Huitzilopochtli, and places it in tandem with the warrior Chicana, who stands as a contemporary figure in a genealogy that situates her as the inheritor of a long revolutionary tradition of women of Mexican descent: Malintzin, Magonista, and Adelita. By joining these two symbols on her canvas, Barbosa metaphorically situates the past with the present. Her warriors are *mujeres y hombres,* men and women, who draw from traditional and egalitarian values.

Dawn announces its arrival with vivid colors whose light allows the viewer to see that there are other objects in the farthest portion of the background. Are those objects more cacti? Are they buildings in the village that this woman came from? Did the woman embark on the pilgrimage to the mythical place that Barbosa refers to in her opening statement? Just as Huitzilopochtli led the Aztecs from Aztlán to Tenochtitlán, is the hummingbird leading the Chicana out of the desert to a new future? It is to Barbosa's credit as an artist that she does not feel compelled to paint neat and tidy visual responses to the queries that an audience might bring to her work. Instead she allows the viewer to ponder the possibilities, just as the female figure in her painting is doing.

Her second work, the black-and-white reproduction of *Chiapas Madonna,* shows a mother embracing her child; the child, in return, is lightly touching her cheek. Although both have their eyes closed, each displays a great deal of tenderness on her face. The Madonna has a truly monumental body. While it is difficult to ascertain her size beneath her draped gown, her exposed arms and neck indicate that she is an amazon. The child's size indicates that she will grow up to be at least as large as her mother is. Barbosa said that she had studied the works of Francisco Zuñiga, a great contemporary Costa Rican–Mexican sculptor, and her oil pastel follows in his style and tradition of portraying the Mexican figure in mammoth proportions. Her portrayal of Mother Earth as Madonna reflects her expressed artistic intent, to tell "stories of innocence, beauty, and passion."

Laura Llano

> Painting is a special activity that helps me release creative energy. It takes me to a special place. I enjoy using watercolor because I can get lost in the exploding color as it hits the paper. I try to control the painting, but often the painting controls me. Painting with watercolors is dangerous, unpredictable, unforgiving, and magical.[33]

Laura Llano's work with watercolors reflects her patience, tenacity, and ability to capture the enchanting qualities of living beings. Many of her works are small renderings of vegetables such as chiles, tomatoes, and corn. She also paints large flowers whose multicolored petals, leaves, stamen, and pollen burst forth from the painting's surface. By comparison, the paintings she selected for the catalog are sedate and cautious in the use of color. This might be due, in part, to the fact that at the time of the interview and while the catalog was in production, Llano was emerging from a difficult period that had to do with her work as an artist. A year earlier she had accepted an assignment to illustrate a children's book with twenty-six watercolor paintings. After an intense twelve months of work, she had eighteen of the twenty-six paintings completed, but the publisher felt this was not sufficient and canceled her contract. Llano explained:

> I had a real challenge last year. I had a deadline and didn't meet it. I've never considered myself an illustrator of children's books, and accepting this contract was like the challenge of my life. I kept saying to myself, What more can I do? For a whole year I had sleepless nights. I'd wake up at three in the morning and just tremble, and say, Oh God, what did I get myself into? Can I ever do this? In the end, I felt like I had let a lot of people down and that my talent had let me down.[34]

As a result of the pressures of her unsuccessful try at book illustration, at the time of the interview she had not painted in watercolor for more than a year. The canceled book contract caused Llano to try oil painting:

I'm trying to change to oils, just to experiment. It's like trying to paint with toothpaste. I mean it's just so different, totally different. So I'm learning.[35]

In spite of this difficult experience, her love for working in the medium of watercolor made Llano committed to returning to that pleasure:

I need to go back and make peace with watercolor because there's an immediate joy there for me. You put that water down, and the color jumps out at you and it bleeds and blends and it's just, well, it's magic.[35]

Painting is an important part of Llano's life because it provides an outlet that alleviates her personal stress and anxiety. She has said that this makes her paintings distinct from political or social art:

My art is therapy for me. It's a tranquil, calming, nurturing thing for me. I choose to paint objects, not make political statements. I choose to paint portraits, still lifes, flowers, and things like that. I appreciate other people's political art, but I don't have this burning desire to be political in my artwork. I don't do political art, but I do broker political thought when I'm teaching.[37]

Llano chooses to bring her cultural politics into the high school classroom, where she teaches Spanish:

I make my students aware of things like the farmworker march in April [1993]. Also, for Día de los Muertos we build an altar in the room. I bring my grandmother's picture, a statue of a Mayan prince, candles, and the whole thing. And since I'm a storyteller, I use a lot of those skills in the class. I'll dress up like Frida and wear a rebozo, paint a single eyebrow on my forehead, wear my hair in a braid. Then I'll be in character, all day, talking to the students as though I were Frida, telling them about my art, my life with Diego, all that. I'll also show them slides of Frida's paintings, or altares that people have made for Día de los Muertos.[38]

Llano's watercolor *Self-Portrait in Paradise* is the painting she selected for full-color reproduction in the catalog. It was created before her turmoil over the book contract and reflects a peaceful moment in her life. The painting is an aerial view of ocean waves lapping onto a shoreline that after a brief stretch of sand becomes totally covered in green waves of foliage. A face emerges from the point where the sand and ocean meet. It is, as we know from the title, Llano's countenance. The ocean's waves are large, and their crests suggest strength in the water below, but they arrive gently on the shore of the sandy beach. The beach is narrow, and its color softly reflects the impending green jungle composed by a series of firmly applied brush strokes. Llano's face reflects the ecological spaces it occupies. Her full lips are blue, their shape almost suggesting the form of a small, delicate vessel being carried ashore by the water, with the placement of her nostrils so close to an approaching wave that she almost breathes in the ocean water. The color of her broad, flattened nose shares the blue qualities of the sea, as well as the muted green of the beach. Her eyes match the subtle green of the forest but are not as bright in tone. It is a quiet work, subtle in its depiction of the tropical setting. Its environment is not one to which the viewer can travel. It exists solely in the mind of and for the pleasure of its creator—the artist. Llano's *Self-Portrait in Paradise* exemplifies her description of how watercolor allows her to get lost in the exploding color. She literally has become one with the watercolor in this work. Llano has painted herself into the environment and, in doing so, is one with the earth and sea.

Another of Llano's watercolors, *The Gift,* is the black-and-white plate in this collection. The painting depicts a hummingbird approaching a blossoming cactus whose uppermost leaf is formed as the profile of a woman. The hummingbird occupies nearly three quarters of the painting's frame, as it gracefully approaches and hovers above the offered cactus blossom. The form of the cactus-woman falls off the right margin of the painting, but the thrust of her face and the direction of the two flowering cactus leaves serve to push the plant back onto the paper. *The Gift* is a gesture to the qualities that Llano perceives as forming the essence of watercolor work—dangerous, unpredictable, unforgiving, and magical.

Villarte commitment, holding brushes in my hand, pushing paint on canvas bland, mental struggle, love and hope, we rise above and cope, where is it found but here? . . . Chicano art . . . an ongoing flow of spicy statements . . . education . . . petal by petal, cultural history and vibrant diversity blossom into people's proud heritages . . . humanity . . . east coast/west coast, warmth and support, life's experiences, north/south American folk art, impressionists/expressionists . . . prison art . . . abstract realism . . . family . . . the child needs to know, am I a part of this village?[39]

For more than thirty years, Helen Villa has been involved in the Chicana/o community of Sacramento. She is wholly embraced as a full member of Co-Madres Artistas, although she is not of Mexican or Latina but of European descent. Her acceptance in the community is rooted largely in her sustained activism and spirit of caring for Chicanas/os and the culture. That Barbosa thought to call Villa with an invitation to exhibit in the originating show, which purported to highlight the work of Chicana artists, is indicative of her status in the community. When queried about her role, she responds, "It doesn't really get brought up that much. I respect the fact that it shouldn't be an issue and the Co-Madres have always not made it an issue."[40]

Villa's family is the focus of her life. When she is not occupied with the daily tasks of cleaning, shopping, and cooking, she is busy handling the administrative details of her artist-husband, Esteban. Esteban is one of the cofounders of several Chicano art groups throughout northern California, including the Royal Chicano Air Force. He is a brilliant, prolific artist whose works are remarkable for his use of color and for their humorous political jibes. Villa says of their working relationship:

I do a lot of the organizing of Esteban and his art exhibits. I try to make sure that everything is on schedule. It doesn't require a lot of paperwork or organization. [When someone calls with a request to exhibit or for the sale of a painting,] he will usually turn the phone over to me and say, "She'll take care of the details." I enjoy doing that. It keeps me busy, and I really appreciate that he includes me in his work.[41]

Because she is a well-organized and community-minded person, Villa's logistical work enables others to be successful.[42] In addition to the attention she gives her family and Co-Madres Artistas, she is also involved in neighborhood issues:

> The neighborhood that we live in is very needy. We have a lot of crime. We don't have a supermarket. We don't have a place for our teenagers. We don't have enough jobs for our community. We are always the last ones to get anything. It's been this way for years. I feel that a lot of work needs to be done here. We are building a community center, and I've played a small part in that.[43]

However, constant attention to the details of other people's lives makes it difficult for Villa to find time to paint in her studio:

> To have my own time to do my own painting means thinking only of myself, and I always manage to think of some task that needs to be done before I think of my own artwork. That process makes it hard to get out there [to the studio] and do it. Rather than take little bits and piece of time throughout the week, I'd rather just sched-ule a long block of time and work through the night. I am learning to work with other people around.[44]

When she does enter the world of her painting she chooses the members of her family as her subjects:

> I basically deal with portraits of family members, my grandkids, and my children. I've tried to cover all of the family. I painted my hus-band and two sons in a triptych. I did my mother, and I'm trying to do my father, but I don't have a lot of pictures of him. A portrait of my dad hasn't really evolved yet.[45]

It is not surprising that the two paintings that Villa chose for the catalog were portraits of her family. *Joseph,* an acrylic work on canvas, shows her toddler grandson seated, curiously examining a watering can on a deck, while behind him are two bentwood chairs. The sun must be nearly over-head because the color of the areas where the sunlight strikes is bleached out, devoid of any subtleties in color. However, Joseph's face is downturned just enough so a shadow falls on his curly head, chubby checks, and smooth forehead. Villa forms her shapes with strong, wide strokes of color, a style reminiscent of Esteban's. She calls attention to detail by placing contrasting colors next to each other, such as in Joseph's hair, whose curls are formed by short, thick swaths of orange, blue, and brown.

The vibrancy of her palette causes the colors to explode from the surface of the canvas. In *Joseph* she limits the range of colors but elaborates on their hues and tones by working a series of gradations that are echoed throughout the work. The cobalt blue of Joseph's shoes in the foreground is found in the middle-ground shadow to one side of Joseph, in his hair, and as a series of shadows in the extreme background of the painting. The bright yellow of the watering can also forms the shape of the chairs, as well as a smaller unrecognizable object in the extreme background. The shape and color of the red tag on the front of Joseph's overalls is echoed in the mouth of the watering can. The can's side is painted with the red, flying chiles logo of the RCAF, an image that Esteban designed.

Her second work in the catalog, *Rene, Esteban, and Nathan,* is the acrylic on canvas triptych to which Villa refers in her opening statement. Its subjects are Villa's husband and two sons. Esteban, in the center, is at an outdoor pay phone, while Rene stands to his left, waiting for him in front of a wall that appears to have been tagged many times over. Nathan, on the right, seems to be at a construction site as he stands on scaffolding with his hard hat, but he is at the site of a mural in progress, one of Esteban's. The quality of the reproduction in the catalog gives the work the feel of a photomural, although the soft focus in which the figures are rendered gives a dreamlike quality to the painting.

Villa's opening line of her artist's statement captures the conundrum that she faces with her desire to paint and to serve her family and community. She is unwilling to forsake one priority for the other, yet she struggles to find time to paint and accomplish her other creative work. When the interview took place she had not begun a new painting in some time and was unsure if she would be able to do so in the near future. But she was clear that her involvement with Co-Madres Artistas had benefited her work as an artist. As a result of her work in the collective, she thought more about ideas for future paintings, had established studio space for herself, and had exhibited more in the last three years than she had in decades. She was hopeful about her future as an artist:

> I really feel good about being a member of the Co-Madres, and I hope it will help me get off my butt and paint more. I really feel like

the group helps me direct my energy into my art and into accomplishing something.[46]

MAREIA DE SOCORRO

Art nurtures the spirit, enhances our visions, and expands our horizons.[47]

For many years before her affiliation with Co-Madres Artistas, Mareia de Socorro enrolled in art classes, co-owned an art gallery, and considered herself an artist. In spite of a vigorous schedule that includes working part time, renovating a historic home in downtown Sacramento, and managing housemates, Socorro is one of the more prolific members of Co-Madres Artistas. And although her schedule is still very full, it is not what it was previously:

Before I joined the group, I was too busy. I was working full time in mental health. It was very demanding. I was doing outreach for the county, and I had a lot of acute cases, child abuse, suicide, and murder. Art was the last thing on my mind because you don't just say to yourself, I'm gonna paint, and that's it. It's not something you can toss off in five-minute increments. You have to live with it, at least that's what I do.[48]

Socorro consistently has new works of art to exhibit at each of the Co-Madres Artistas' shows because she is willing to experiment with a variety of media and techniques:

You know, I do an acrylic, finish it, and want to move onto something else. So I do a charcoal. And then I'm through with that, I'll do mixed media. I don't stay in one medium. I have to be challenged.[49]

Socorro paints for her personal pleasure. The choices that she makes regarding materials, subject, and technique are all predicated on her desire and creative impulse at the time that she is initiating a work:

I want it all. I work three days a week sometimes so that I can do art. I turned down full-time work so that I can paint. Painting is like a privilege to me. It's a high! I do it for myself. When I paint something, I'm pleasing me. If nobody ever saw my work or bought it, it wouldn't matter to me.[50]

However, Socorro actively markets her paintings. She feels strongly about retaining possession of her original art:

I want to market my work. But, you know, I won't sell my originals. When people ask if they can buy my original works, I tell them, "I will sell you a high-tech print, but I will not sell the original."[51]

The representations in Socorro's works span a wide range of subjects. Many are related to Chicana/o culture. Some paintings are indicative of her interest in the prehistoric cave paintings of Europe, and other works reflect her love for children. Her job requires her to work with abused children. She wants her art to communicate the need to create a more caring environment for children:

Children are really the message of my art. I feel like children throughout time have never had sufficient protection. That they survive amazes me. With all the brutality that children face, I'm amazed that the human race didn't phase out long ago. I titled one of my paintings *Hope: Children of the World*.[52]

Both of the paintings that Socorro selected for the catalog celebrate everyday aspects of Chicana/o-Mexican culture. The full-color plate is a reproduction of an acrylic painting, *The Curtain Rises on Mole*. A woman sits on a blanket with her back to the viewer as she grinds some of the many ingredients that it takes to create the Mexican dish *molé*. She is arduously grinding the ingredients using her *metate*. Her hard work is evident in her stooped shoulders as she moves the pestle up and down the face of the mortar. The cook is oblivious to the fact that a curtain made of flaming red chiles and yellow corn has been lifted, and she is now exposed to an audience. The curtain has a life of its own as the chiles wriggle furiously toward one corner and the corncobs roll and lumber along on the opposite side. Next to the cook are piles of garlic, nuts, and cinnamon sticks. Socorro's colors are rich and enhance the smells that are hinted at in the cook's use of so many pungent ingredients. She paints in varying shades of red and yellow and mixes the two colors into a vibrant saffron shade for the blanket on which her cook sits.

Socorro's other contribution to the catalog is a charcoal, *The Deer Dances.* It is fairly common for at least one deer dance, Indio Yaqui Danza del Venado, to be on the performance bill of a Mexican ballet *folklórico.* The dance invokes the indigenous Mexican ritual of the Sonoran Desert–based Yaqui. In Socorro's rendering, the male dancer wears a large mask with tall horns and little else save for a loincloth. His face is entirely covered, and he hunches over so as to mimic the figure of the deer. Socorro has captured well the animal-like form of this deer dancer by shaping his torso and forearms so that they closely resemble those of a deer. It is unclear if the light in the upper right-hand corner is a spotlight or the luminescent moon. The dancer could be onstage or in a field. The dancer's ambiguous setting extends to his stance, which might be a leap, suspended in midair, or poised on one foot, preparatory to a leap. The dancer is filled with the spirit of the deer as he cavorts across the page.

With the aid of Co-Madres Artistas, Socorro has stretched as an artist. In addition to exchanging ideas with the other members, she makes it a point to attend concerts as well as lectures on archaeology in an effort to build on the inspiration of the collective. She remains constant in her commitment to creating art that "nurtures the spirit, enhances our vision, and expands our horizon."

Collective Success: "We Belong to the Community"

Co-Madres Artistas' work has met with a great deal of success as a result of the catalog. On average, they have collectively exhibited in five shows per year over the past decade. They have individually exhibited in many more shows. The Co-Madres Artistas have embraced the complexities of working together as members of an artistic collective. Early on they faced the challenge of understanding and working with each other's personal and creative expectations of the group's function as an art-producing organization. Their first exhibition highlighted some of the dynamics that bless and problematize the group's processes. By working together on the same exhibition opportunity, the women of Co-Madres Artistas alleviated much of the pressure that arises from solo exhibitions. By agreeing to a group show, they were able to handle logistical matters, as well as personal and creative pressures, collectively. Because all of the artists were returning to the studio, they were able to encourage each other. Working against the deadline of an exhibition gave the members a time frame within which to accomplish their artistic goals.

Lucy Montoya Rhodes, the collective's administrator, is the person most credited for their early successes. She coordinated the group's activities and was responsible for fulfilling the reporting requirements of the California Arts Council grant. Her efforts permitted the artists to focus on their cultural work. Castillo recalls Montoya Rhodes's contributions from that early period: "She was the glue that kept us together. She did so much then. She still does. She calls us up and asks what she can do."[53] Montoya Rhodes's contributions, while numerous, were pointed out to me by the artists and not by Montoya Rhodes herself. She is humble about her organizational leadership. Castillo remarks on this characteristic of Montoya Rhodes: "Lucy is a stoic person who believes in herself. She doesn't need to self-promote to feel strong."[54] Although she later changed her mind, Montoya Rhodes asked me to exclude her from this project:

I think you should exclude me. The manuscript is about the art. I helped them to put on the art shows. . . . [I was] another person helping to take care of the many, many details of putting on a show. I helped them with the grant from the California Arts Council; I was the support staff. I coordinated the writing and submission of the required reports. . . . [A]ll that work is done [now]. I am not the administrator of the group. I am their number one fan and sup- porter-helper, that's all. I know they love me and appreciate my help. That's enough for me.[55]

Some situations have tested the group's capacity for resolving differ- ences. Two of the artists came to the collective with a history of acrimony. Each of these members was interviewed and spoke on condition of anonymity about the tensions between them. Each also made a point of acknowledging that their fraught relationship was in the past. It is clear that these artists have broadened their understanding of each other through their work in Co-Madres Artistas. It is testimony to their commit- ment to the group that they have placed the success of the collective above previous disagreements.

Another complicated dynamic emerged during the first year of the collective's life. It was typical for the opening party of Co-Madres Artistas' exhibitions to include a ritual blessing. Usually the ceremony was led by Josie Talamantez, the group's spiritual adviser, or chaplain, as they called her. She invoked a blessing of the four directions with smudge pot and candles and asked that the exhibit, the artists, the audience members, and the community at large be endowed with good health, fortune, and opportunity.[56] In addition to the invocation, another celebratory character-istic of Co-Madres Artistas' exhibitions was the inclusion of an altar-installation. Various members of Co-Madres Artistas contributed to the creation of the installations. But not all members viewed the altar-installations as necessary components of the exhibitions. This difference of opinion was manifested most sharply in a discussion that took place as a result of the 1993 exhibition, *Historias de Esperanza/Stories of Hope*. Barbosa created one of the more elaborate altar-installations for this show. She explains:

> I made this huge sculpture of an altar, authentic, the way you find them in Mexico[,] you know, where abandoned buildings have fallen apart, and the people poke holes in the bricks, and use the door-ways to put their relics and pictures. To get to the altar, you had to walk through a sculpture. . . . [T]hey were the open legs of the Mother Earth giving birth to the Sixth Sun. . . . [H]er vagina was lit up, her eyes were flaming, and she was holding, on high, this bundle of eagle feathers.[57]

Castillo, who spoke a great deal in her interview about the ways in which she weaves her spirituality and her artistic representations, is careful not to name the artists involved in this debate:

> Some of the girls don't want to participate in having our altars. They think it's religious instead of cultural. At first the altars were kinda pushed on us and some didn't like it. Now some of the exhibits have altars and others don't.[58]

Socorro's view is that the altar-installations are vehicles for communica-ting family history and group culture:

> Altares are different things to different people. I think they make a connection with our family and ancestors. You know you can take

all of these courses that tell you about other cultures, and yet it never gets pointed out that we have cultural tradition[s] here, in our homes, too.[59]

Llano describes herself as a religious person and views the ceremonies and altar-installations as tributes to God. They enhance her connectedness to the art and the creative process. She also understands that other members do not share her feelings:

I am a religious person. I don't go around proselytizing or convert-ing or anything. However, I am religious. I have an eclectic view of God. I know that He's there. However, any way anyone wants to worship Him is fine with me. If someone wants to do a Japanese tea ceremony or blow smoke in the four directions, I will work with that person. I will join in because I think God loves diversity. God loves the infinite, the creative, and is probably bored to tears with the same old ceremonies.[60]

This debate is viewed as a thing of the past, and members look to the future instead because they derive strength from their commitment to each other. Their covenant as artists and activists working together collectively underscores their longstanding role as leaders in the Chicana/o Art Movement.

In July 2002 Co-Madres Artistas celebrated their tenth anniversary with an exhibition of paintings, prints, multimedia displays, and photography at La Raza Galería Posada, their home gallery in Sacramento.[61] The exhibition, *Co-Madre Enchiladas: . . . Diez Años,* was a celebration of their success as a collective, their ongoing work in the community, and their personal commitment to their work as artists. The exhibition also served as testimony to their roles as *comadres.* Theresa Harlan describes the conscious extension of Co-Madres Artistas' positioning as comadres, as women of Mexican descent committed to providing for those in their immediate circle and for members of the community at large:

A significant element of the ideas and concepts carried through the work of the Co-Madres Artistas is their decision of how to identify themselves as a group. The selection of Co-Madres Artistas goes beyond a means of identification and accurately represents the years of experiences of nurturing family and community and the demonstrated commitment of the Co-Madres to their community through creative expressions.[62]

In the Mexican kinship tradition of the comadre, the members of Co-Madres Artistas provide a metaphorical and a material bounty that is dispersed to a broad circle of family, friends, and artists. Their role as comadres also extends to their activism in the Chicana/o community of Sacramento, where their social awareness and involvement provide the inspiration for their artistry. Socorro frequently reminds her Co-Madres that the symbiotic nature of their relationships with one another and with the Chicana/o community contributes to their strength as a group: "I tell them, 'Solo, we are not that important. But as Co-Madres, we are giants.' We belong as a whole to the community."[63]

Notes

1. Among the participants in the first exhibition were Irma Lerma Barbosa, Carmel Castillo, Laura Llano, Katherine Garcia Smith, and Helen Villa. Mareia de Socorro was invited but could not participate because of a hand injury.
2. Lucy Montoya Rhodes, personal communication, November 8, 2001.
3. Laura Llano, interview, July 25, 1994.
4. Mareia de Socorro, personal communication, August 7, 2001.
5. This description is borrowed from Irene Blea's characterization of Chicanas from this generation of women. Irene I. Blea, *La Chicana and the Intersection of Race, Class, and Gender* (New York: Praeger, 1992), 65.
6. RCAF materials are archived in the special collections department of the library at the University of California, Santa Barbara. This archive contains valuable information about the group's contributions to the Chicano Art Movement, including works of art on paper and primary and secondary source materials. The latter contain references to Chicanas' help in sustaining the RCAF, including a mention of Irma Lerma Barbosa's photographs documenting the group's mural work. In addition, a number of Chicana artists, including Celia Rodríguez, Lorraine García, and Carol Hernández, are credited for their artistic contributions to the RCAF's murals in Sacramento and San Diego.
7. Helen Villa, interview, June 15, 1994.
8. Irma Lerma Barbosa, interview, July 25, 1994.
9. Carmel Castillo, interview, June 15, 1994.
10. Laura Llano, interview, July 25, 1994.
11. Irma Lerma Barbosa, personal communication, July 19, 2002.
12. Lucy Montoya Rhodes, interview, August 22, 1994.
13. Mareia de Socorro, personal communication, August 7, 2001.
14. Lucy Montoya Rhodes, "Co-Madres Artistas Grantee Self-Evaluation for the

California Arts Council Multi-Cultural Entry Grant Program" (1993). Each member in the group was required to respond to the CAC's self-evaluation form.

15. Helen Villa, "Co-Madres Artistas Grantee Self-Evaluation for the California Arts Council Multi-Cultural Entry Grant Program" (1993).

16. *Co-Madres Artistas: Story/Visions from the Cactus Tree: A Catalogue of Fine Art* (Sacramento: California Arts Council, 1994).

17. Esteban Villa, "Introduction," in *Co-Madres Artistas: Story/Visions*, 3.

18. Theresa Harlan, "Co-Madres Artistas: Making a Name for Self and Community," in *Co-Madres Artistas: Story/Visions*, 4.

19. At the time of publication, Socorro used her surname, Zuñiga; hence her placement in the order of names.

20. Carmel Castillo, *Co-Madres Artistas: Story/Visions*, 7.

21. Carmel Castillo, interview, June 15, 1994.

22. Ibid.

23. Ibid.

24. Ibid.

25. Ibid.

26. Irma Lerma Barbosa, *Co-Madres Artistas: Story/Visions*, 11.

27. Irma Lerma Barbosa, interview, August 22, 1994.

28. Ibid.

29. Founders José Montoya and Esteban Villa were veterans of the Korean War and attended college on the GI Bill. While studying art at the California College of Arts and Crafts, they formed the Mexican American Liberation Art Front (MALAF). They formed the Rebel Chicano Art Front, the RCAF, when they were reunited as teachers in Sacramento. The abbreviation, the same as that of the Royal Canadian Air Force, was the occasion for many jokes. Irony was frequently the locus of the group's artistry and emerged in different forms. One example is the group's reworking of their name to the Royal Chicano Air Force. The group's visual and performance artistry are legendary, and its members have contributed greatly to Chicano aesthetics over the past thirty years.

30. Irma Lerma Barbosa, interview, August 22, 1994.

31. Ibid.

32. Roberta H. Markham and Peter T. Markham, *The Flayed God: The Mesoamerican Mythological Tradition: Sacred Texts and Images from Pre-Columbian Mexico and Central America* (San Francisco: Harper–San Francisco, 1992), 296.

33. Laura Llano, *Co-Madres Artistas: Story/Visions*, 12.

34. Laura Llano, interview, July 25, 1994.

35. Ibid.

36. Ibid.

37. Ibid.

38. Ibid.

39. Helen Villa, *Co-Madres Artistas: Story/Visions*, 14.

40. Helen Villa, interview, June 15, 1994.

41. Ibid.

42. I can testify firsthand to her abilities and thoroughness. Her eye for detail was wonderfully beneficial to this research.

43. Helen Villa, interview, June 15, 1994.

44. Ibid.

45. Ibid.
46. Ibid.
47. Mareia de Socorro, *Co-Madres Artistas: Story/Visions,* 14.
48. Mareia de Socorro, interview, June 15, 1994.
49. Ibid.
50. Ibid.
51. Ibid.
52. Ibid.
53. Carmel Castillo, personal communication, June 19, 2002.
54. Ibid.
55. Lucy Montoya Rhodes, personal communication, June 17, 2002.
56. Irma Lerma Barbosa, interview, August 22, 1994.
57. Ibid.
58. Carmel Castillo, interview, June 15, 1994.
59. Mareia de Socorro, interview, June 15, 1994.
60. Laura Llano, interview, July 25, 1994.
61. La Raza Galería Posada press release, March 10, 2002.
62. Harlan, "Co-Madres Artistas," in *Co-Madres Artistas: Story/Visions,* 4.
63. Mareia de Socorro, telephone communication, July 7, 2002.

FOUR

Coatlicue's Cartography

Mapping Hybridity and Creative Collectivity

Néstor García Canclini's work on hybridity is useful in this concluding discussion.[1] García Canclini identifies hybridity as an organic formulation resulting from the dynamic that takes place when trajectories of cultural production, social interaction, and symbolic capital overlap. He says of this process:

> Frequently hybridization transcends the simple fusion of discrete social structures or practices that existed separately: by combining, they generate new structures and new practices. At times this occurs in an unplanned fashion, or is the unforeseen result of the practices of . . . communicational exchange. But, often hybridization arises from individual and collective creativity—not only in the arts, but also in everyday life.[2]

The processes and products of Mujeres Muralistas and Co-Madres Artistas parallel García Canclini's ideas regarding hybridization in the ways in which the artists interpolate the quotidian elements of their lives, their interactions with one another, and their relationship to their audience and to other artists in the development of their imagery. Their cooperative envisioning results in visual representations that affirm their identities within the Chicana/o community and serve as their aesthetic expressions of resistance to mainstream constructs. We see in the stories of Mujeres Muralistas and Co-Madres Artistas how their collective organization permits the development of creative projects whose imagery transcends the boundaries of their individual positions as artists, as women, as Chicanas, and as active participants in the Chicana/o Art Movement. García Canclini is again useful in understanding the ideological imagery of Mujeres Muralistas and the entrepreneurial character of Co-Madres Artistas:

> [H]ybridization initiated as a sociocultural movement . . . can be converted into products that enact recognition of the exotic or the reconciliation between cultures in a transnational market. Innovative aesthetic constructions can become market operations.[3]

Mujeres Muralistas enacted such a reconciliation of cultures through their murals, which express a vision of a distinctly Chicana/o-Latina/o community whose cultural boundaries are flexible and whose permeability allows for many forms of identification to travel within and through the parameters of the significations. The artists were clearly self-conscious about reflecting the cultural diversity of Chicanas/os and Latinas/os in their murals, and the accuracy of the traditions that their imagery represents was important to them. Because each artist was responsible for designing and painting a specific portion of the mural and because that work was created outside, on the street, the artists were held directly accountable by the public for the images they created.

Co-Madres Artistas' representations are less sharply influenced by the formation of the group than are those of Mujeres Muralistas. Because Co-Madres Artistas members work individually as easel painters, they are able to develop their separate styles without the necessity of group negotiation. However, their drive to consistently exhibit their works as a collective effort requires a cooperative spirit. Co-Madres Artistas make their impact as a collective in three areas: providing one another with personal encouragement and creative problem-solving skills, acquiring ongoing exhibition space, and securing outside funding. Co-Madres Artistas' development as an entrepreneurial collective within the socially conscious atmosphere of the Chicana/o Art Movement evokes the dynamism of hybridization:

> Hybridization is more than a simple overcoming that denies and conserves that synthesizes opposites; [it] is a field of energy and sociocultural innovation. It can be a pretext for commercial manoeuvres or a support for conversations that inaugurate unexpected visions.[4]

Co-Madres Artistas are able, in large measure, to negotiate their way through seemingly paradoxical situations because of their maturity as middle-aged, working women. As central players in many of the Sacramento Valley Chicana/o arts organizations and social service agencies, which have come and gone over the past three decades, they have learned valuable lessons regarding group processes. The collective also benefits from the stability of its membership. With the exception of one departure after the first exhibition, the membership remained constant until 2002, when another originating member left the group. This stability, as well as the artists' longstanding acquaintance, makes it possible to withstand the pressures of a rigorous exhibition schedule.

Coatlicue's Cartography

The monolith of Coatlicue serves as a marker of the ways in which women artists of Mexican descent are cast aside, buried, and disregarded. The Mexican art historian Justino Fernández situates Coatlicue as the essential figure of Aztec consciousness: "In Coatlicue, Aztec art expressed itself with profound knowledge, for it succeeded in giving form to a complicated concept by means of structures that were logical, geometrical, functional, and symbolic."[5] Through this optic the statue of Coatlicue serves as the inscribed basalt body of Aztec cosmology, intellectual production, artistic expression, and historical knowledge. Fernández describes, moving from bottom to top of the statue, the symbolic implications of the statue's visual elements:

> The legs of Coatlicue are formed from eagle talons, symbolic of the Sun God, and are decorated with eagle plumes. They are covered by a short skirt hemmed with a row of bells, symbolic of thunder, which proceeds rain. In the lower part, at the back, is a tortoise, which alludes to childbirth. The simple interlaced serpents that form the skirt are man, humanity, clinging or dependent on the mother— the earth; but the serpents of the belt whose heads hang down in front are divine, as are all the rest, for their bodies are covered with precious stones. In the middle of the stomach is a skull. Coatlicue is dressed in the skin of a flayed woman, a symbol of spring, and is adorned with a collar of hearts and hands, referring to the sacrifices

necessary for the gods. Further, she is shown decapitated, to sym-
bolize the moon. Coatlicue is a female goddess, and for this reason
is shown with a skirt, the tortoise, and the skin with pendant breasts;
but this divinity is also male, and for this reason a great serpent can
also be seen beneath the skirt, lodged between the legs. Finally, the
dual principle which forms the head not only caps the work but per-
meates everything, whether exterior, to the front, or to the back.
Thus the sculpture of Coatlicue becomes much more than just the
Goddess of Earth or the Goddess of the Serpent Skirt. In effect it
symbolizes the earth, but also the sun, moon, spring, rain, light, life,
death, the necessity of human sacrifice, humanity, the gods, the
heavens, and the supreme creator.[6]

Coatlicue signifies, for Fernández, a series of bifurcated constructs that
exist as co-presence: female/male, human/animal, sun/moon, earth/sky,
birth/death, darkness/light, mammal/serpent, past/future. As a symbol of
cyclical movement, she is the gerundial form: being, becoming, moving,
altering, articulating, gesticulating, birthing, dying, existing, living.
Fernández casts Coatlicue as the embodiment of the spiritual, social, and
cultural landscape of the Aztec people. Just as Coatlicue serves as an
ancient multifaceted signifier of the complexity of being, so do the creative
collectives Mujeres Muralistas and Co-Madres Artistas serve as
contemporary reflections on the lightness (and the weight) of being
Chicana. Mujeres Muralistas and Co-Madres Artistas, like Coatlicue, are
perceived as the aggregation of multiple significations; within a mosaic of
symbols and processes lies their strength as contributors to an aesthetic.
Mapping the complexity of Coatlicue is parallel to mapping the hybridized
artistry and processes of Mujeres Muralistas and Co-Madres Artistas: there
is always something more to be read in the works.

Chicanas' contributions to the visual arts have remained largely unac-
knowledged by Chicano and mainstream art institutions, although Chicano
cultural organizations have been somewhat better in recent years about
foregrounding their works. But the incident at La Galería de la Raza, with
which I opened this book, is an example of how Chicana artistic production
is ignored within the movement. Arrival at the museum is not, however,
without its own problems. Recalling the opening story regarding the installation of Mujeres Muralistas' artwork at the San José Museum of Art
reminds us how the mainstream art world continues to treat women of
color artists as window dressing, particularly those artists who create

expressly political works. This event underscores the ignorance of the main-stream art world and its resulting inability to contextualize and comprehend the aesthetic that emerges from the Chicana/o Art Movement.

As this book began, so it ends, with a vignette. One afternoon, on the cusp of submitting this manuscript to the publisher, the hard drive of my computer crashed. Kaput. Into the netherworld of encrypted fragmentation went some of my carefully scripted ideas. Driving hurriedly to the local computer *brujo*-geek, my journey came to a halt in front of a railroad crossing where freight cars rolled back and forth: left, then right, left, then right, left. . . . As I marked time and sighed with impatience, I decoded the tags on the railroad cars, "Luvah Buoy," "Nuckl Hed," "Anotha one." It took some work, but eventually I made out the words on one of the more baroque tags, "You can't abolish those who astonish."

Immediately, I was reminded of Mujeres Muralistas and Co-Madres Artistas. To be more precise, I was reminded of Graciela Carrillo, Consuelo Méndez, Ester Hernández, Patricia Rodríguez, Carmel Castillo, Irma Lerma Barbosa, Laura Llano, Mareia de Socorro, and Helen Villa. They astonish as they continue to produce exceptional works of art, serve their communities, and provide for their families, and their contributions cannot be abolished.

Never underestimate the tenacity of a Mexican woman.

Notes

1. *Gracias* to Ana Patricia Rodríguez, a generous scholar and colleague, who first introduced me to the work of García Canclini. The following English transla-tions of García Canclini's work elaborate further on the points raised in this chapter: *Transforming Modernity: Popular Culture in Mexico,* trans. Lidia Lozano (Austin: University of Texas Press, 1993); *Hybrid Cultures: Strategies for Entering and Leaving Modernity,* trans. Christopher L. Chiappari and Silvia L. López (Minneapolis: University of Minnesota Press, 1995); "The State of War and the State of Hybridization," in *Without Guarantees: In Honour of Stuart Hall,* ed. Paul Gilroy, Lawrence Grossberg, and Angela McRobbie (London: Verso, 2000).
2. García Canclini, "The State of War and the State of Hybridization," 38–39.
3. Ibid., 50.
4. Ibid., 49.
5. Justino Fernández, *A Guide to Mexican Art, from Its Beginnings to the Present,* trans. Joshua C. Taylor (Chicago: University of Chicago Press, 1969), 45.
6. Ibid., 43–44.

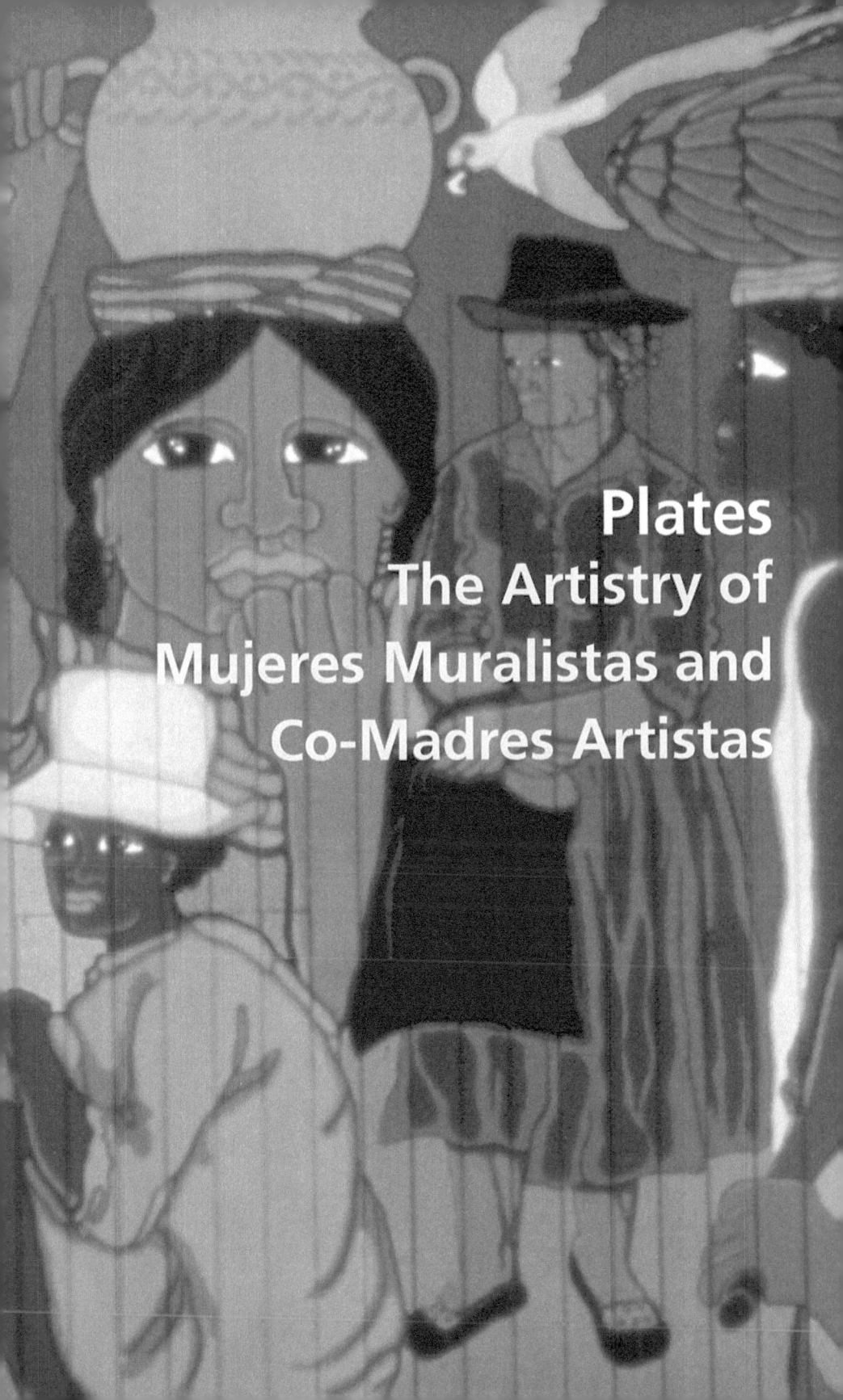

Plates
The Artistry of
Mujeres Muralistas and
Co-Madres Artistas

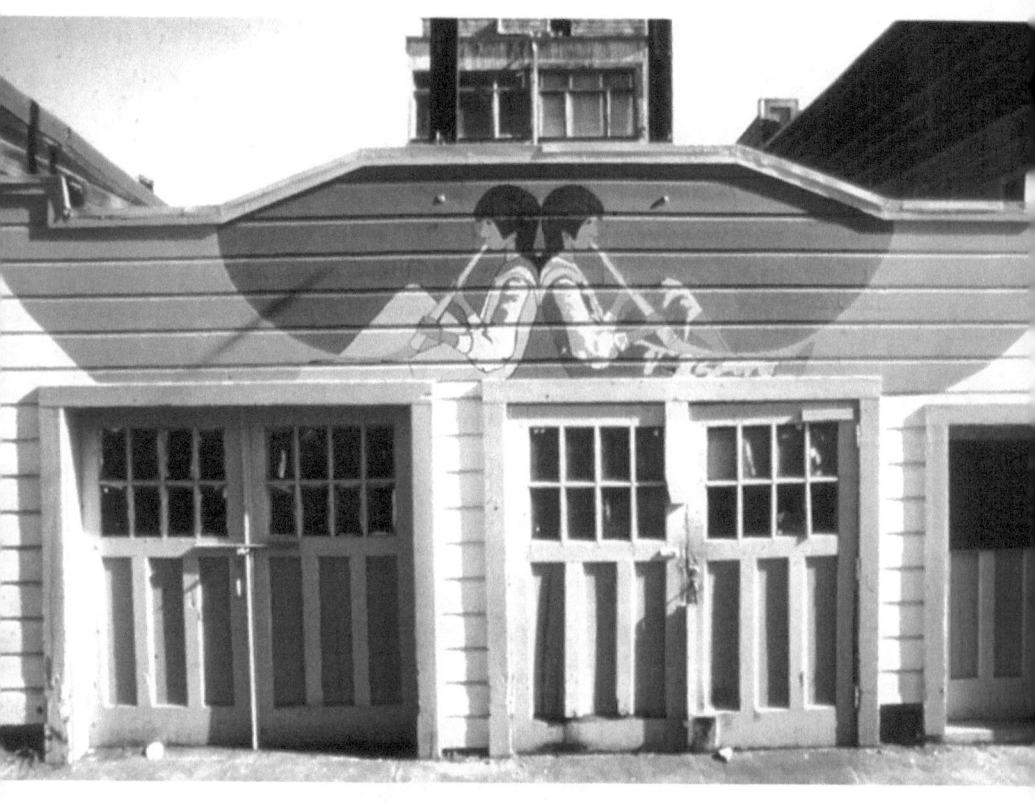

Plate 1 (above). Irene Pérez, untitled Balmy Alley mural, 1973, acrylic on wood. Photo credit: Timothy W. Drescher. Reproduced by permission of the artist.

Plate 2 (opposite). Graciela Carrillo and Patricia Rodríguez, untitled Balmy Alley mural, 1973, acrylic on wood. Photo credit: Timothy W. Drescher. Reproduced by permission of Patricia Rodríguez.

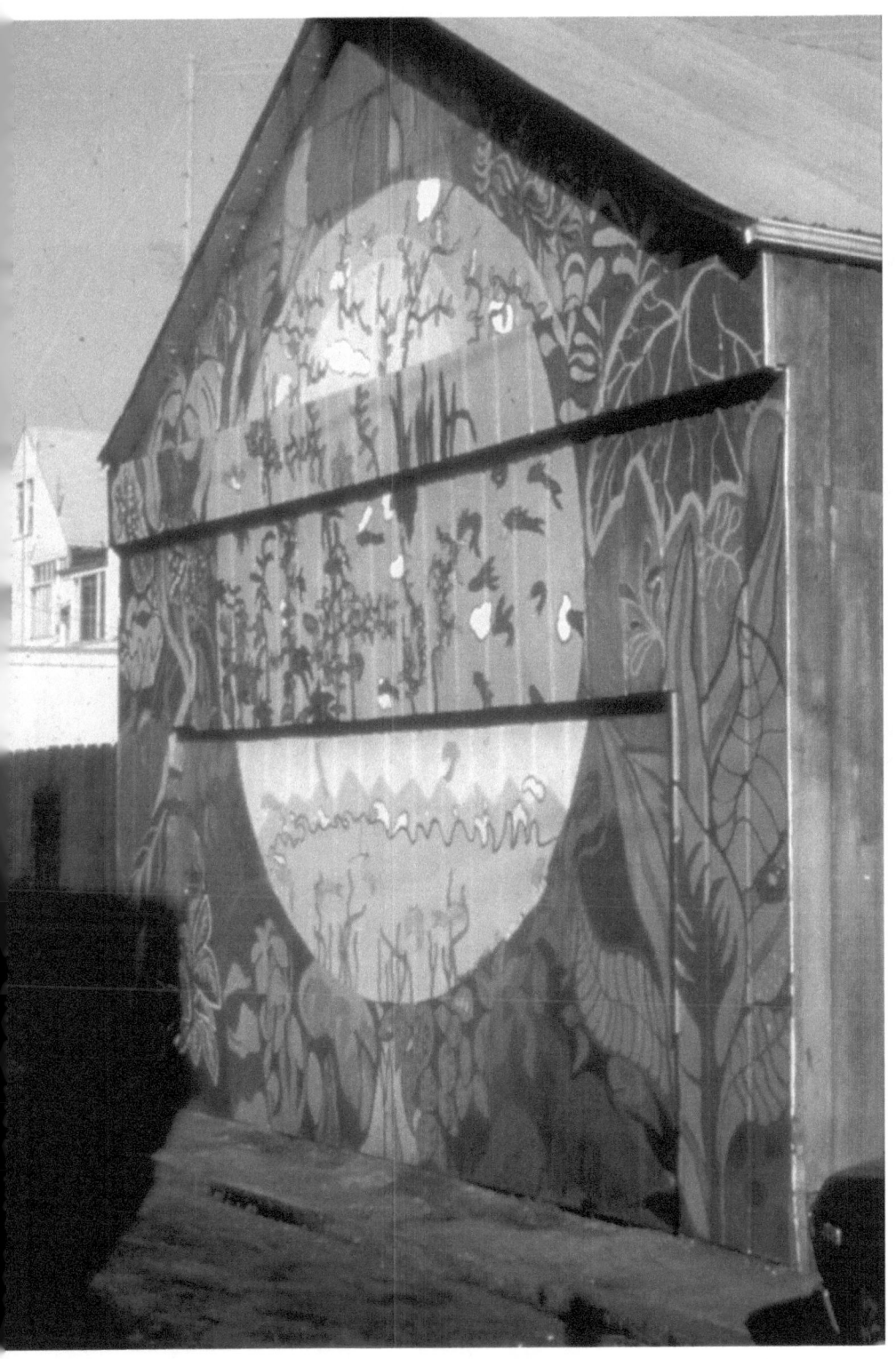

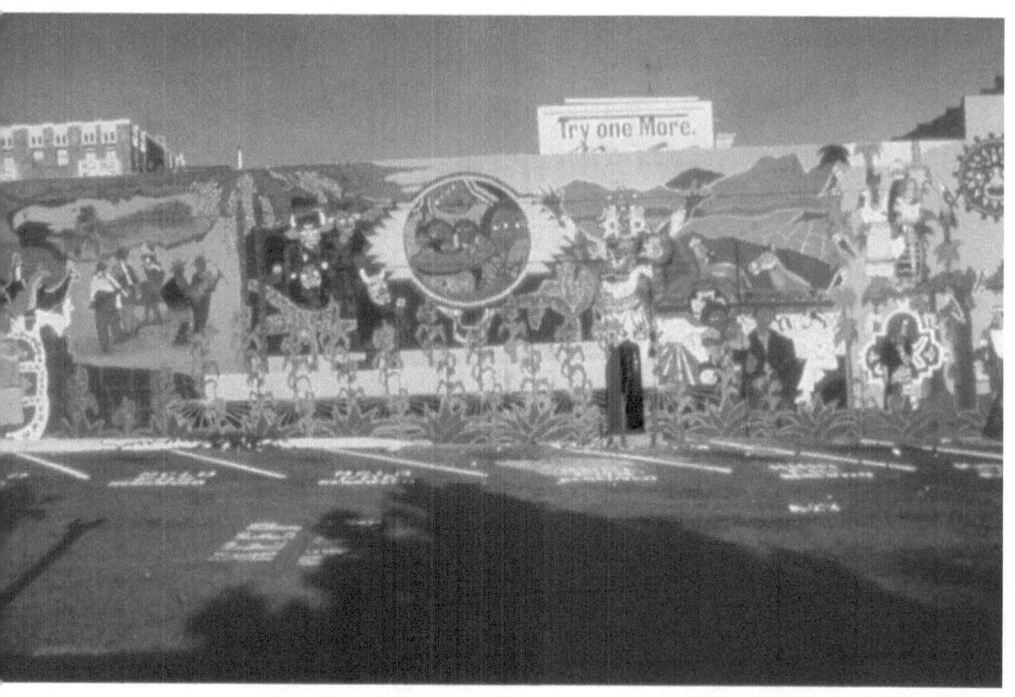

Plate 3 (above). Mujeres Muralistas, *Latinoamerica,* 1974, acrylic on masonry, 20′ x 76′. Photo credit: Timothy W. Drescher. Reproduced by permission of the artists.

Plate 4 (opposite). *Latinoamerica* detail. Photo credit: Timothy W. Drescher. Reproduced by permission of the artists.

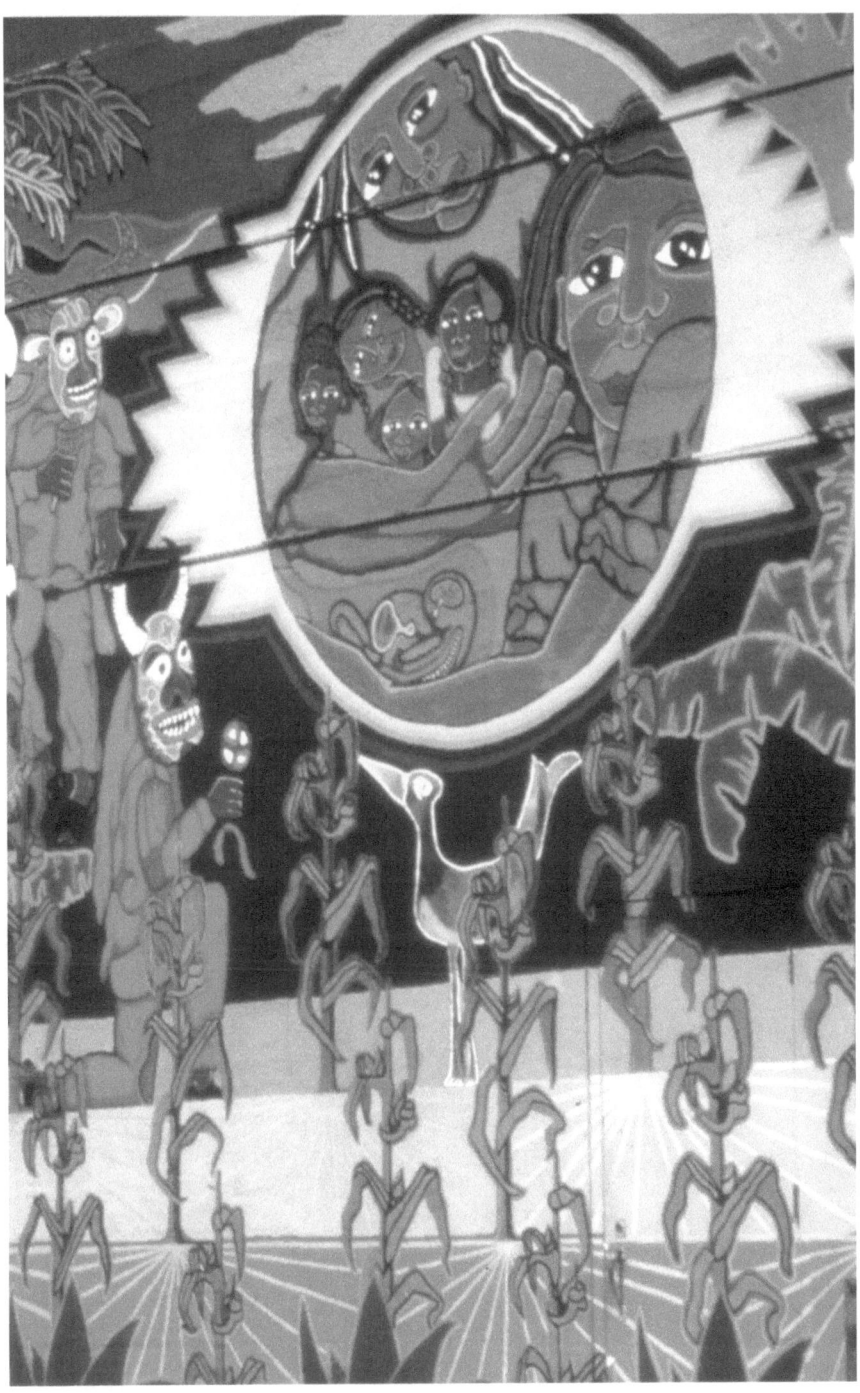

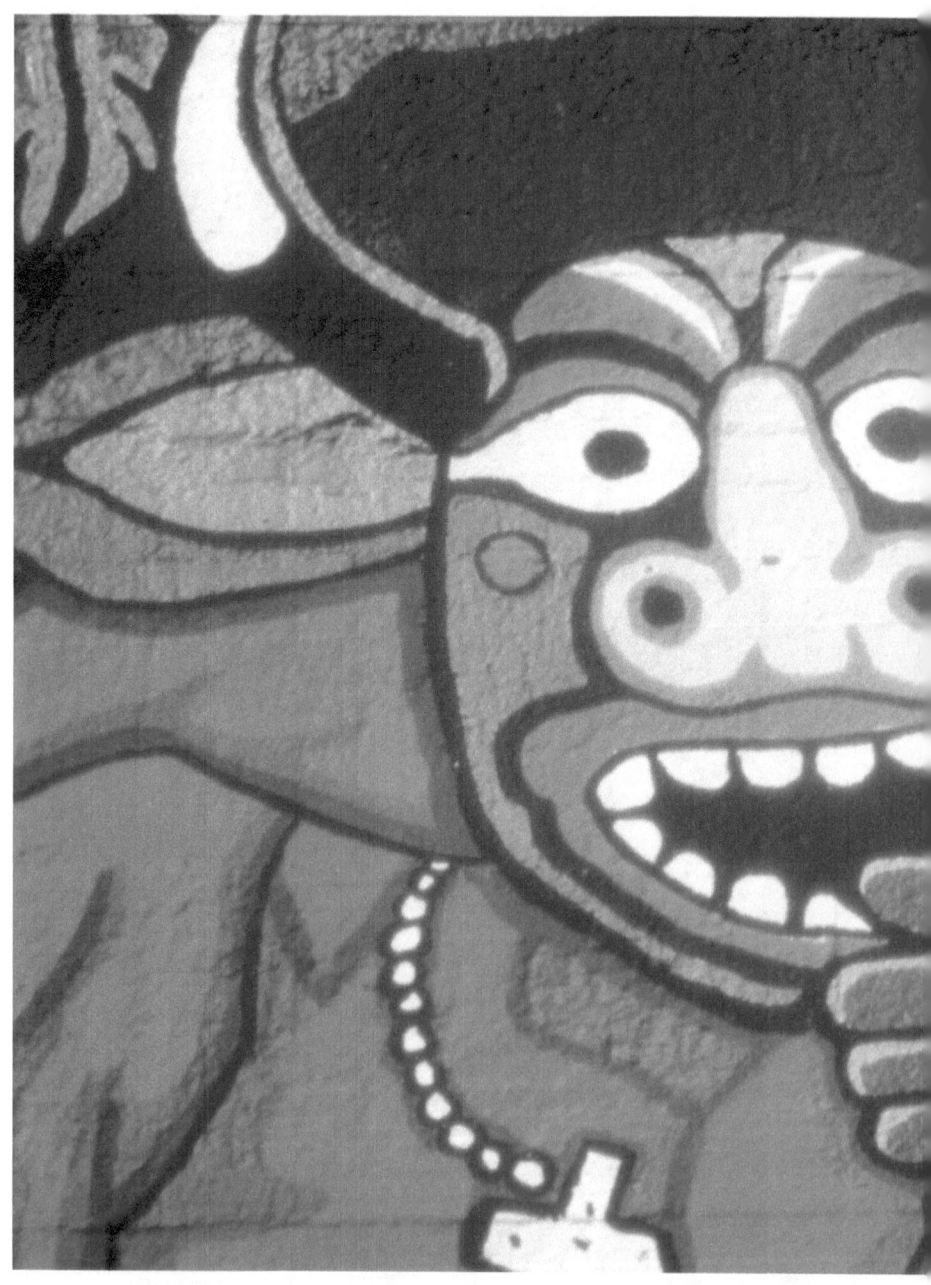

Plate 5. *Latinoamerica* detail. Photo credit: Timothy W. Drescher. Reproduced by permission of the artists.

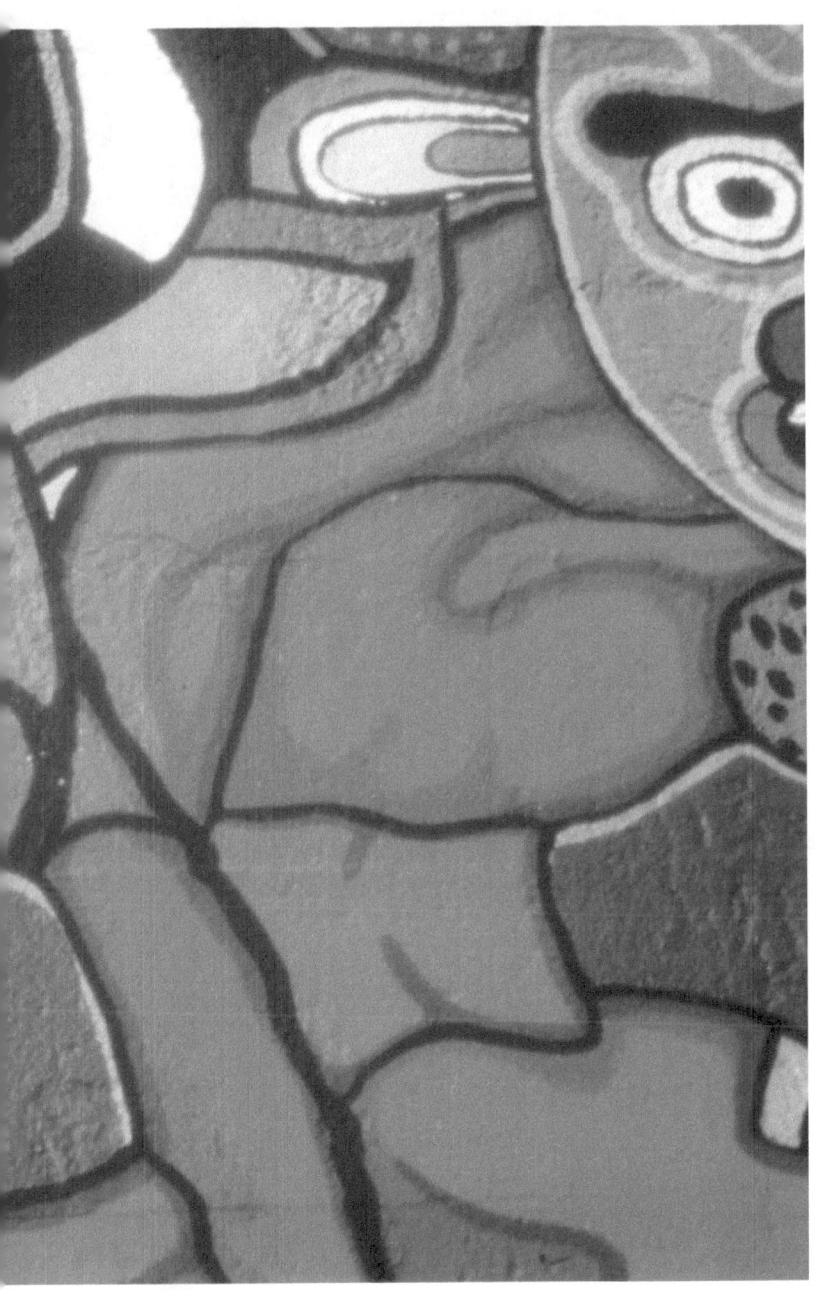

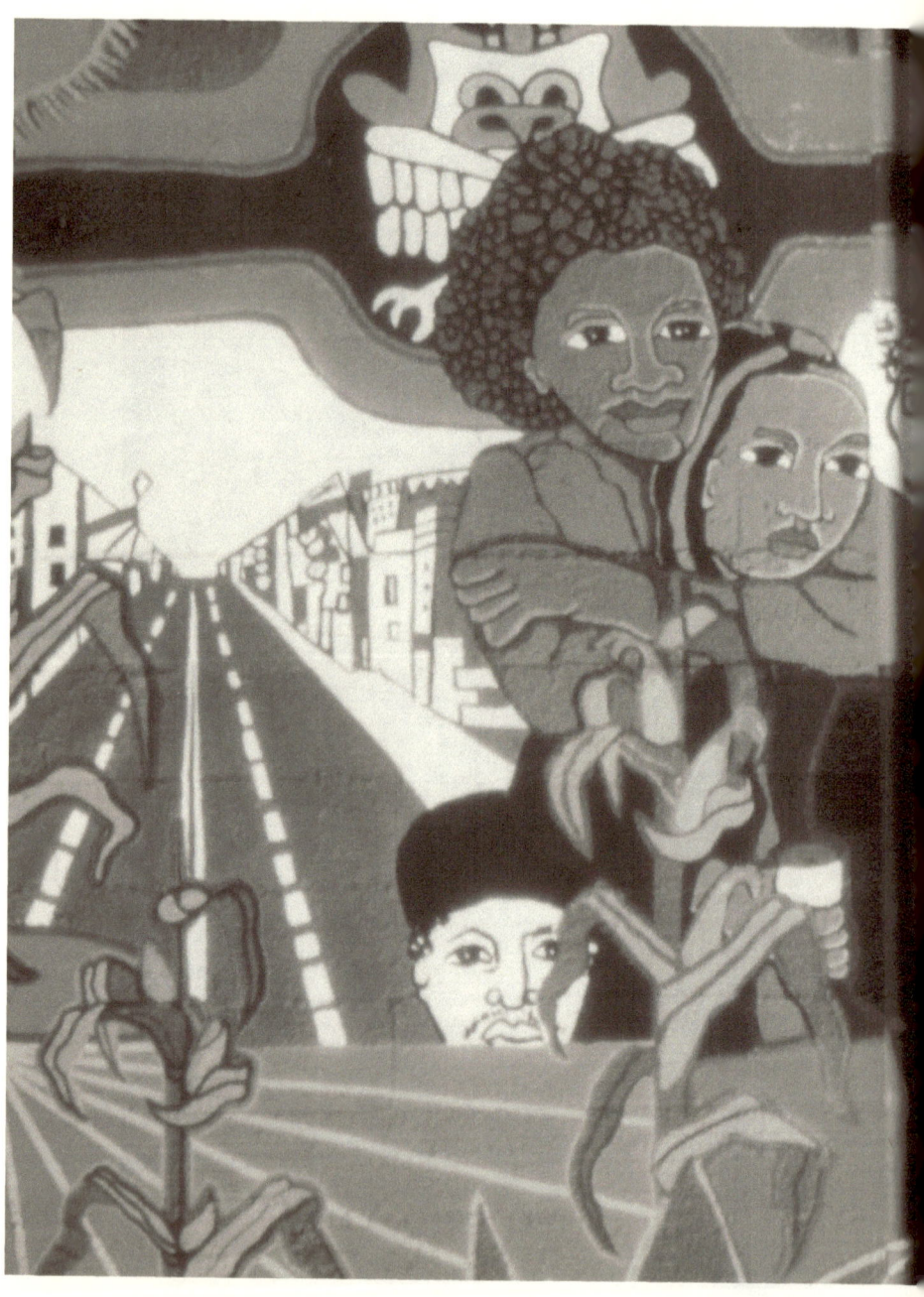

Plate 6. *Latinoamerica* detail. Photo credit: Timothy W. Drescher. Reproduced by permission of the artists.

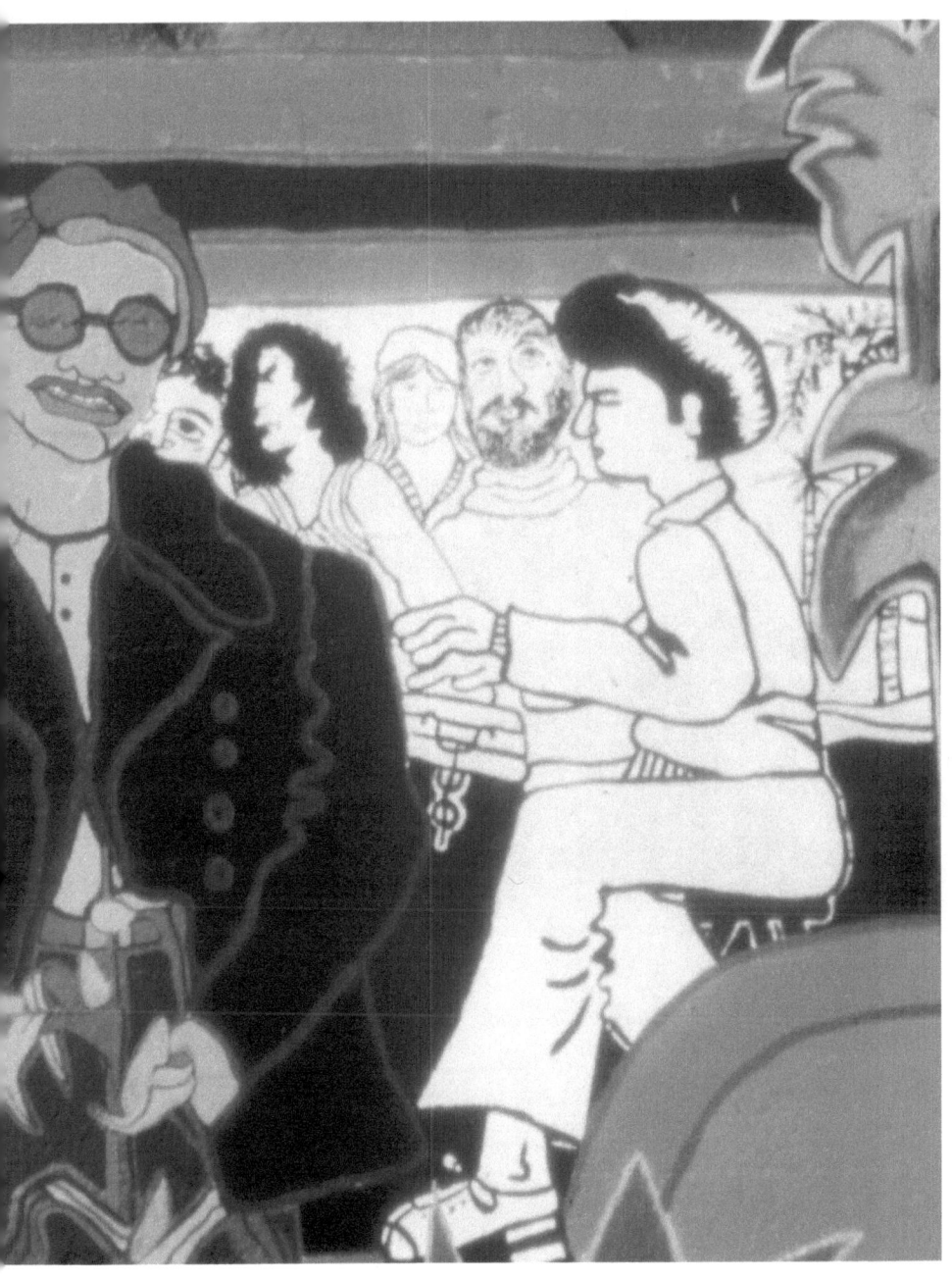

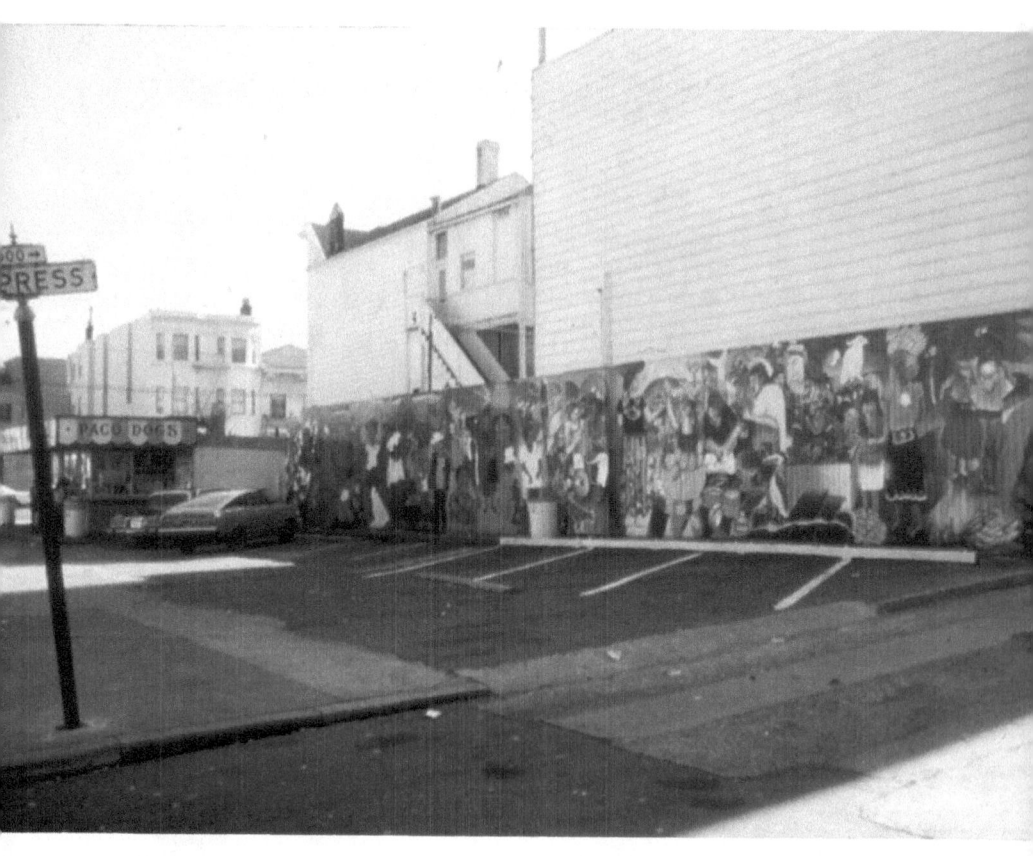

Plate 7. Mujeres Muralistas, *Para el Mercado,* 1974, acrylic on wood, 24' x 76'.
Photo credit: Timothy W. Drescher. Reproduced by permission of the artists.

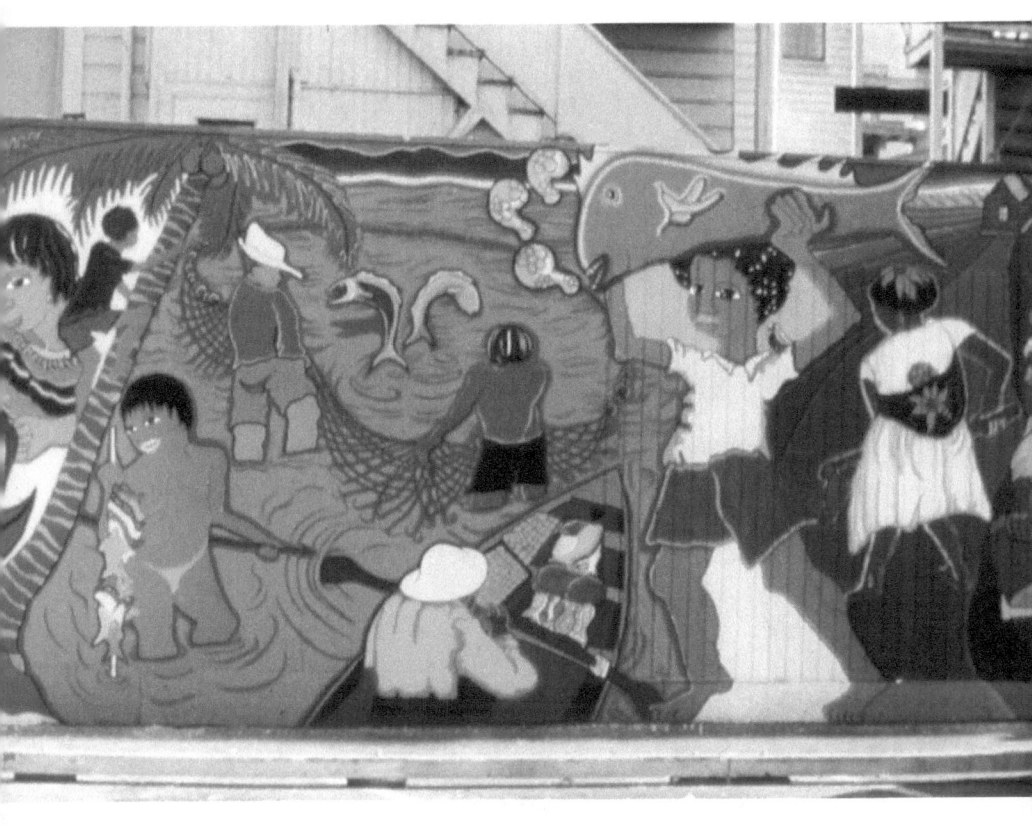

Plate 8. *Para el Mercado* detail. Photo credit: Timothy W. Drescher. Reproduced by permission of the artists.

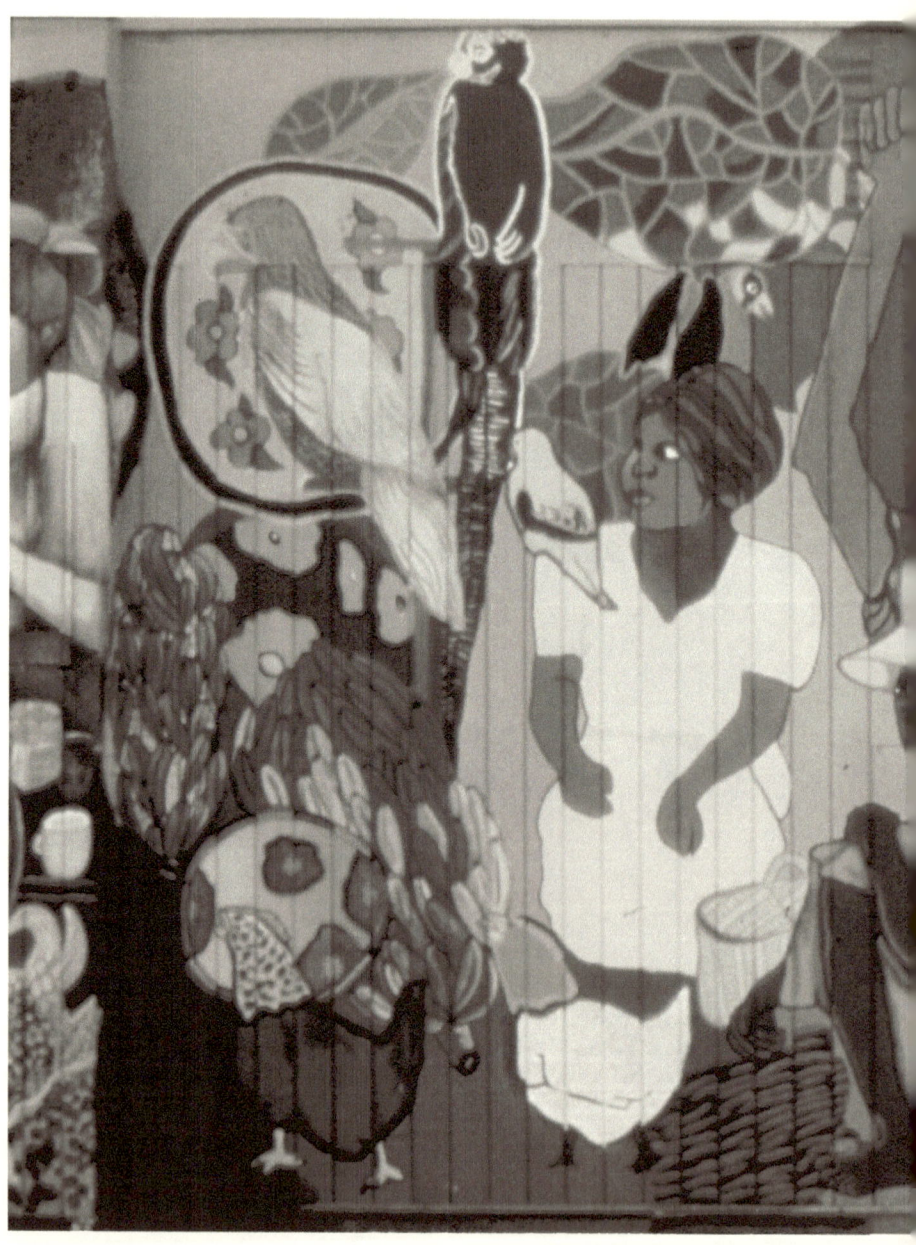

Plate 9. *Para el Mercado* detail. Photo credit: Timothy W. Drescher. Reproduced by permission of the artists.

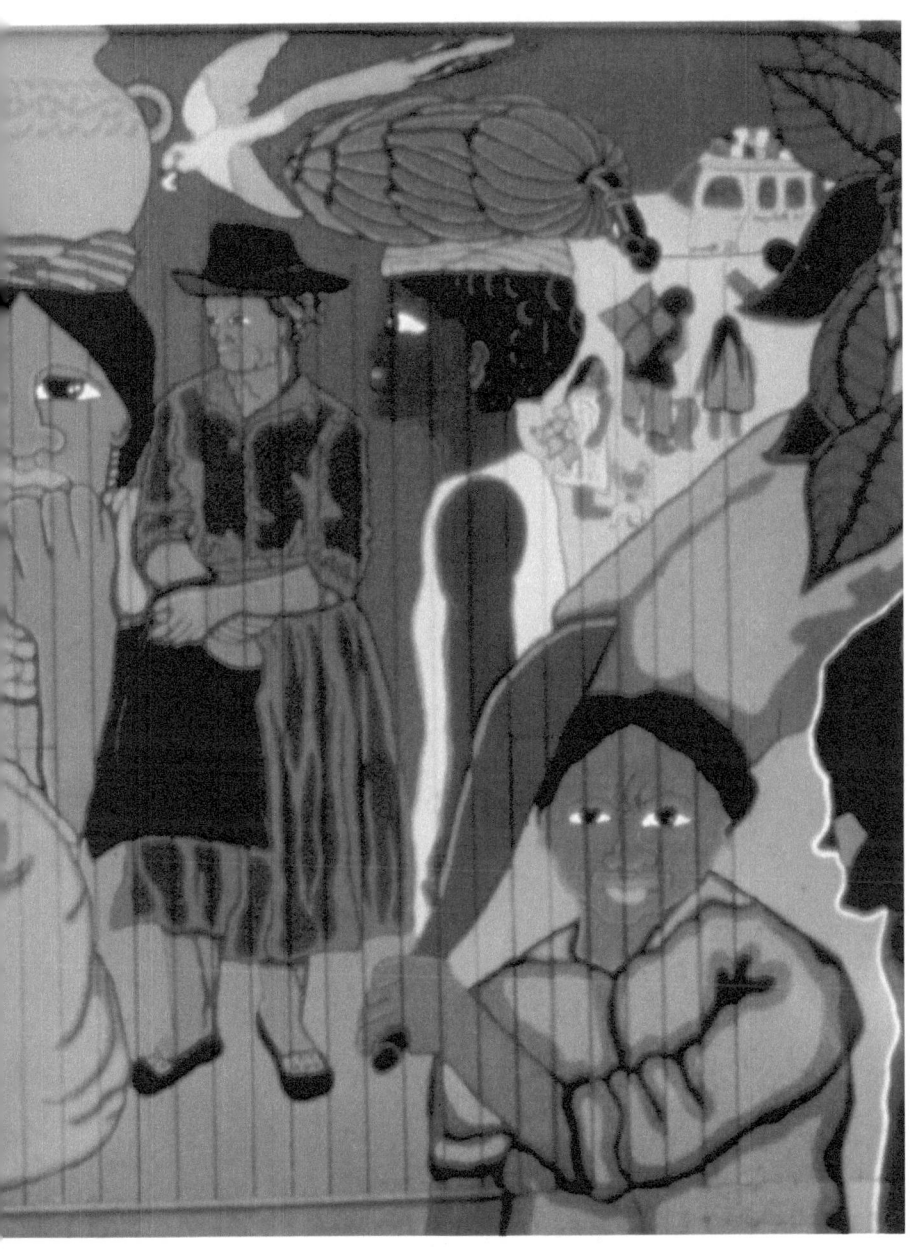

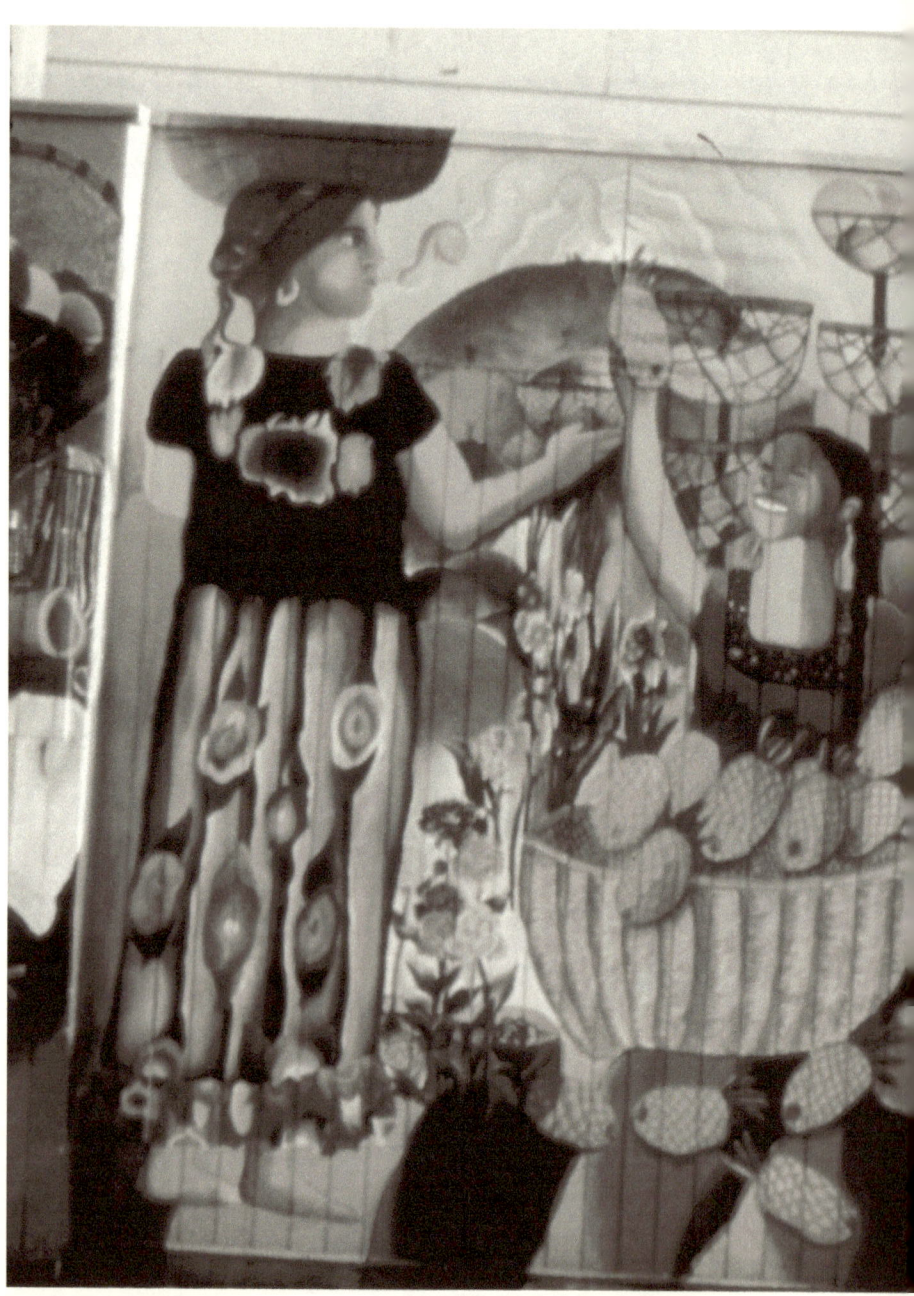

Plate 10. *Para el Mercado* detail. Photo credit: Timothy W. Drescher. Reproduced by permission of the artists.

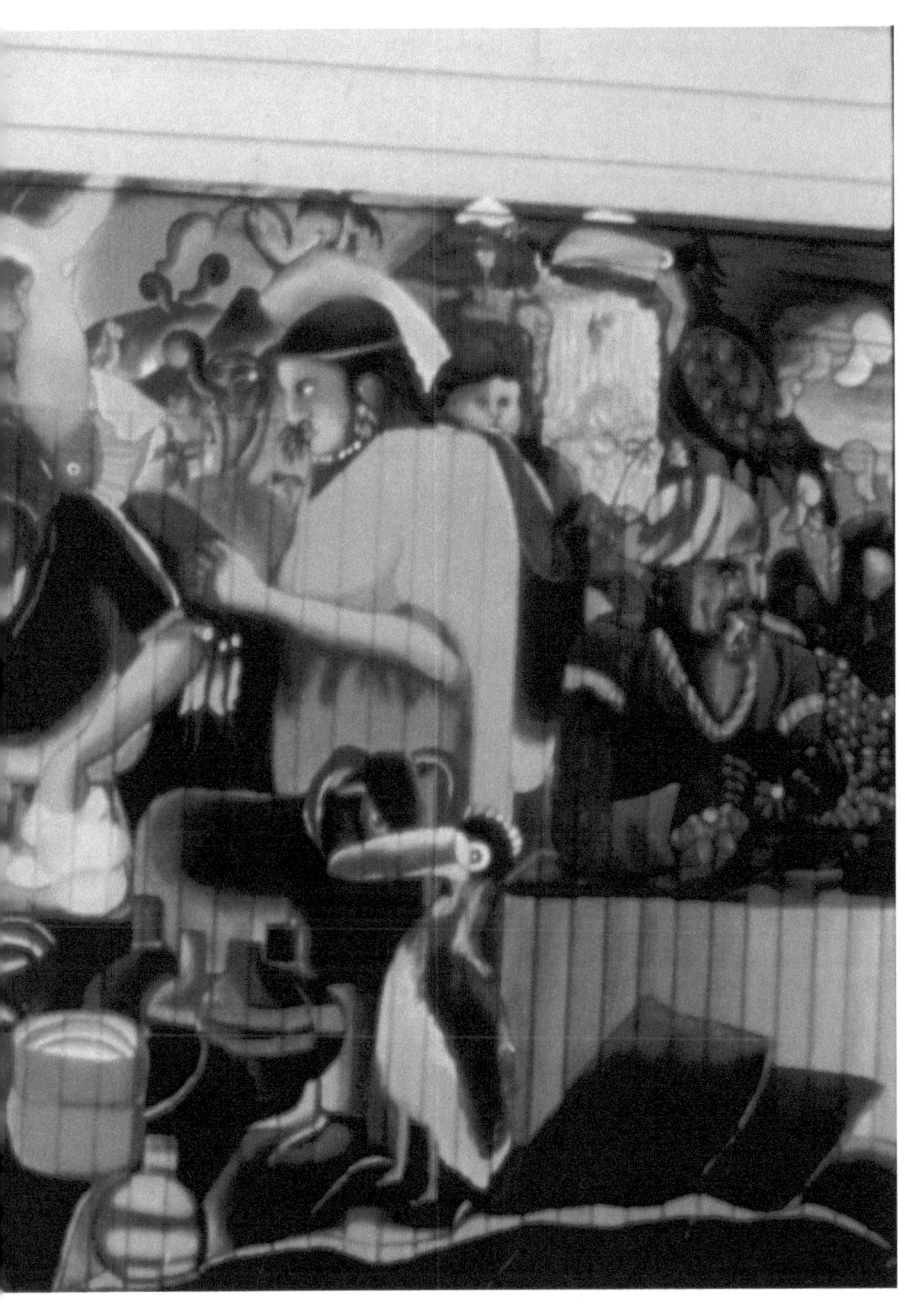

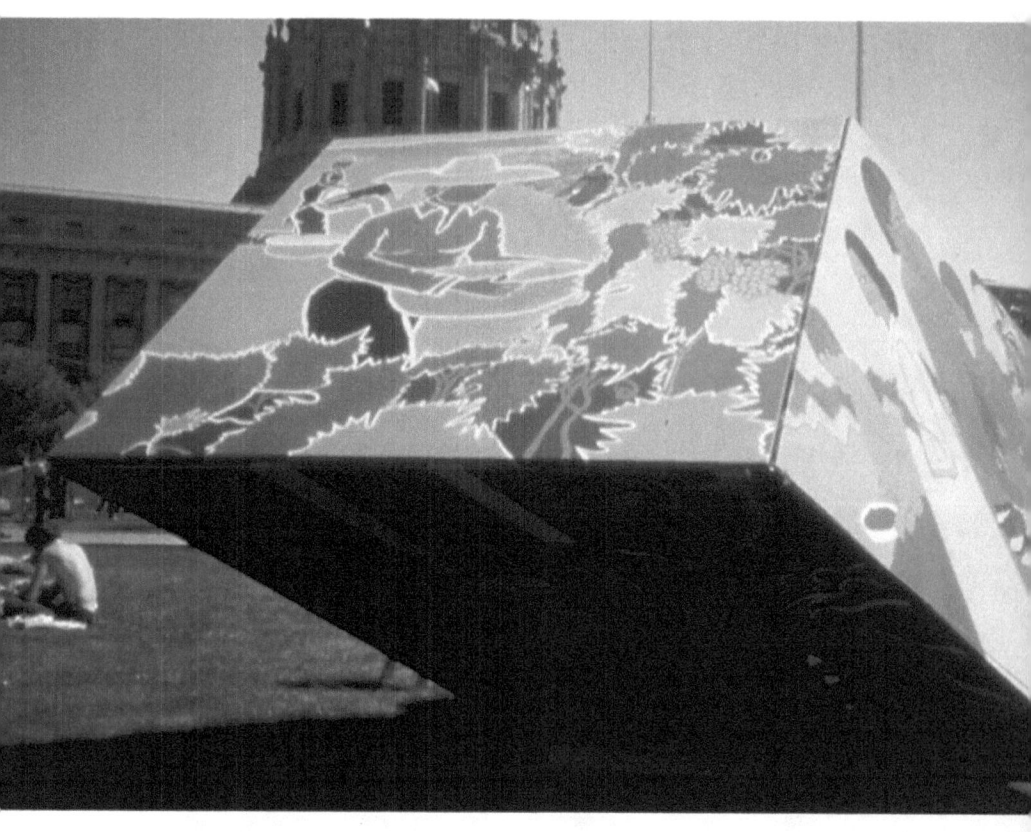

Plate 11. Mujeres Muralistas, *Rhomboidal Parallelogram,* 1975, acrylic on canvas, six panels each 7' x 7'. Photo credit: Consuelo Méndez. Reproduced by permission of the artists.

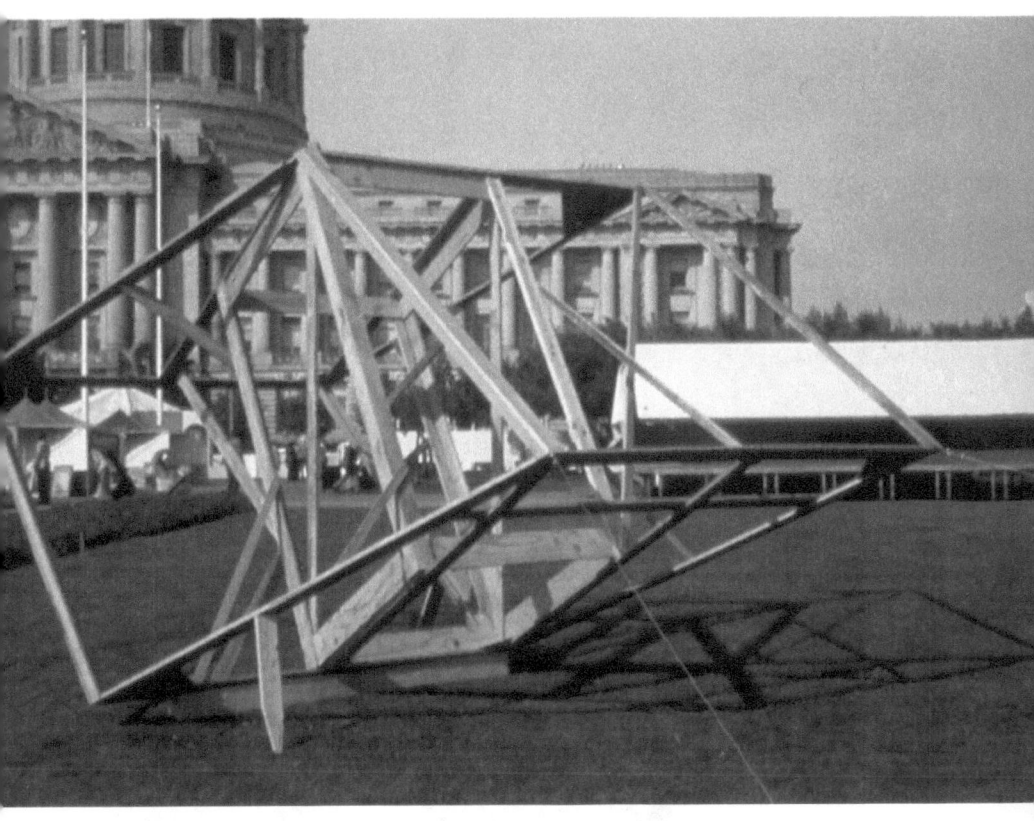

Plate 12. Framing device for *Rhomboidal Parallelogram.* Photo credit: Consuelo Méndez. Reproduced by permission of the artists.

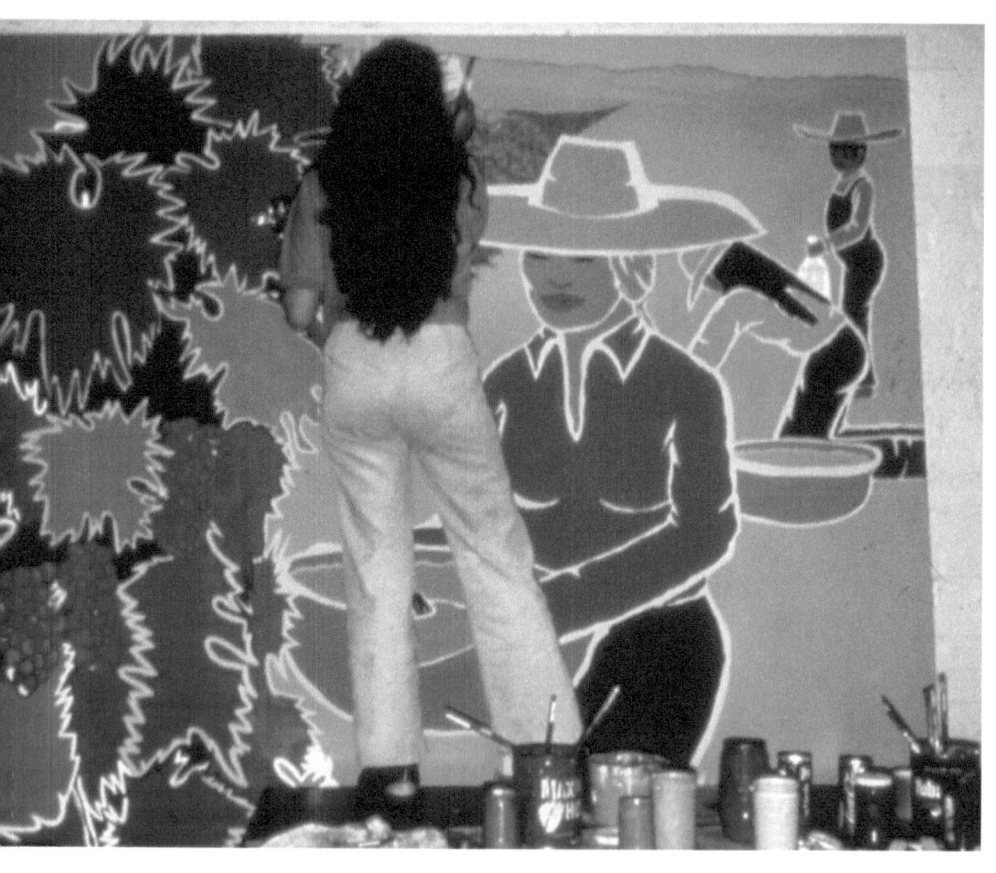

Plate 13. Ester Hernández painting her panel for *Rhomboidal Parallelogram*. Photo credit: Consuelo Méndez. Reproduced by permission of the artist.

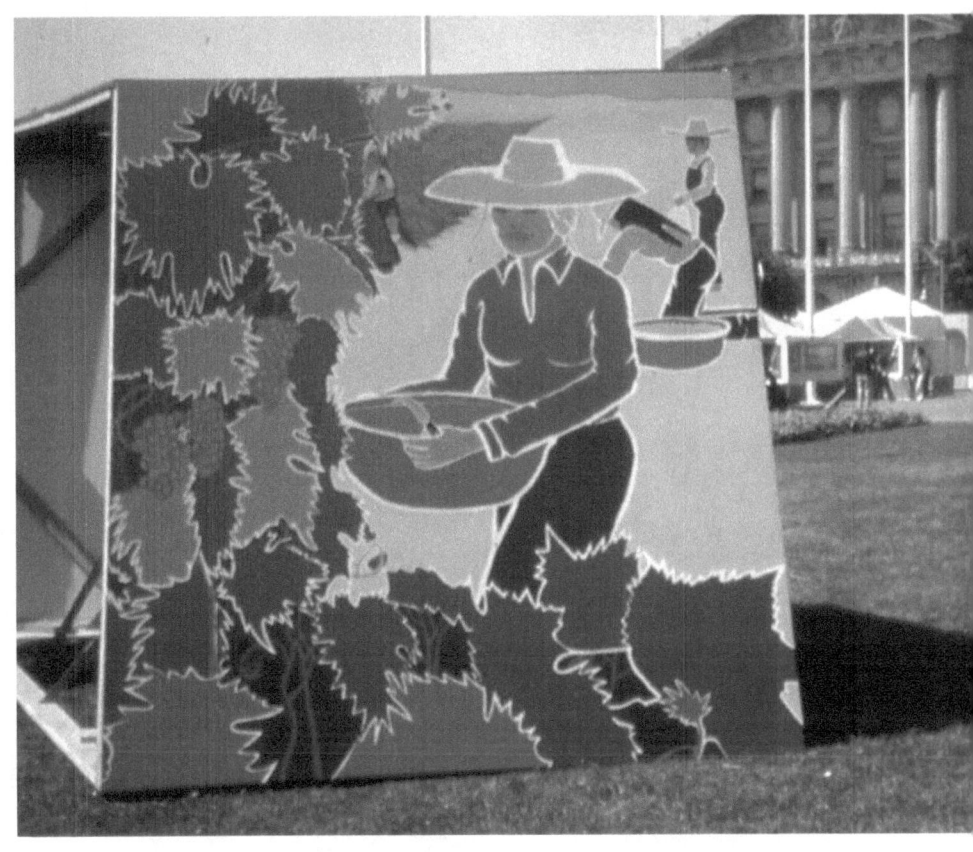

Plate 14. *Rhomboidal Parallelogram*, detail of Ester Hernández's panel. Photo credit: Consuelo Méndez. Reproduced by permission of the artist.

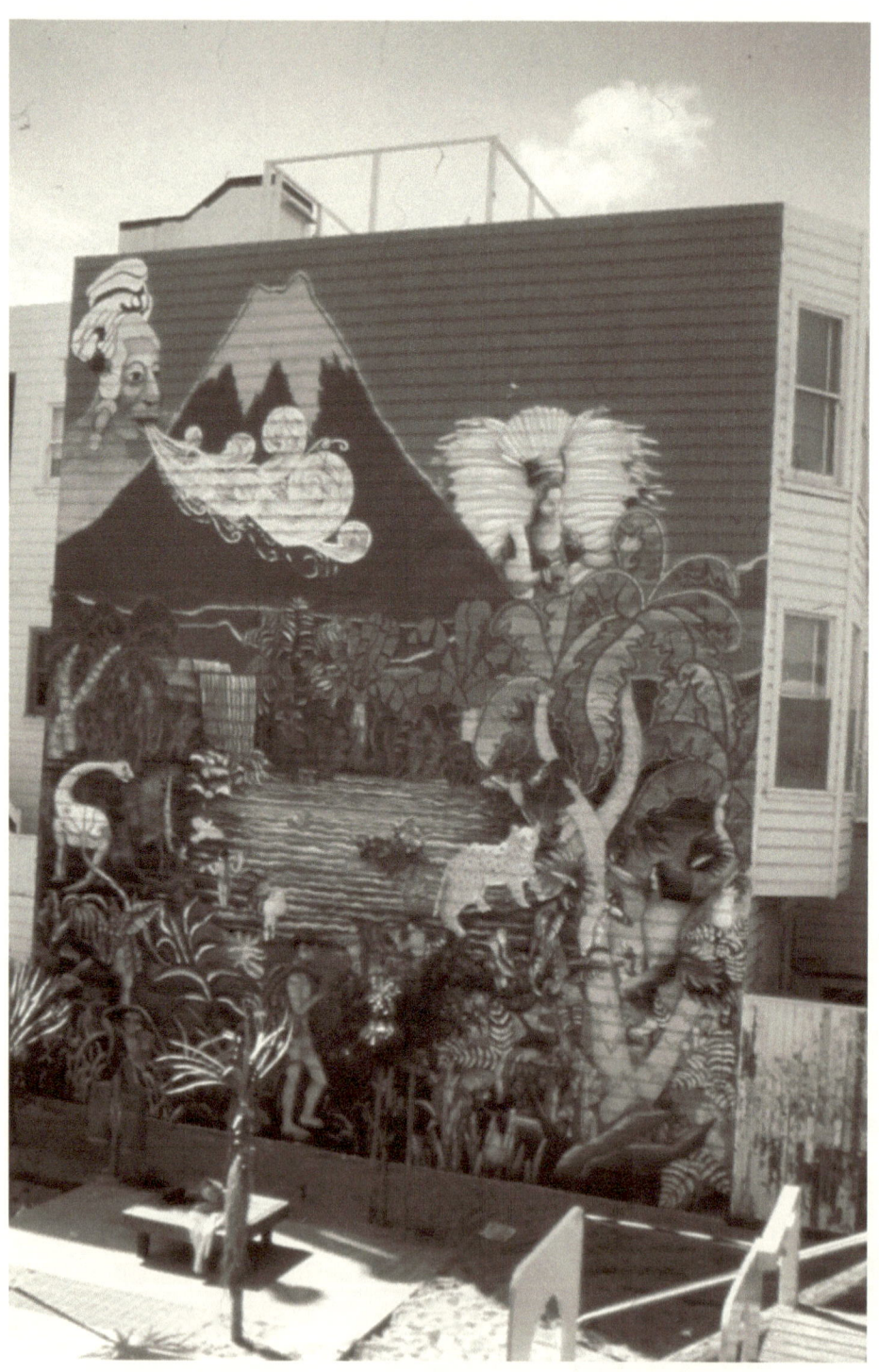

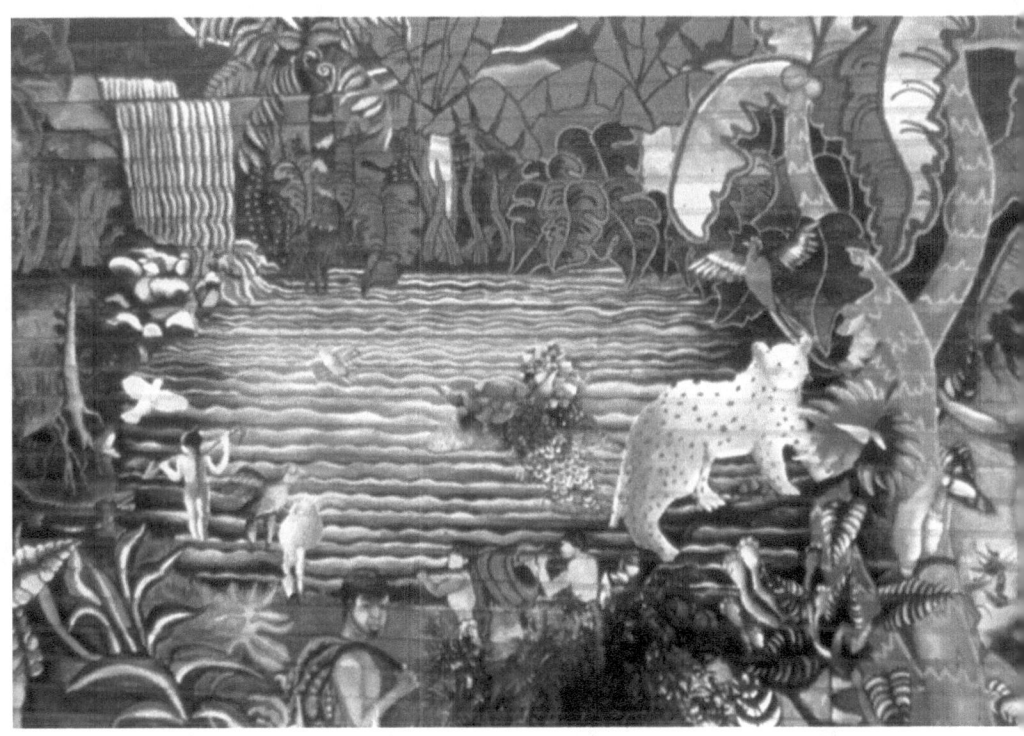

Plate 15 (opposite). Mujeres Muralistas, *Fantasy World for Children*, 1975, acrylic on wood, 40' x 20'. Photo credit: Patricia Rodríguez. Reproduced by permission of the artists.

Plate 16 (above). *Fantasy World for Children* detail. Photo credit: Patricia Rodríguez. Reproduced by permission of the artists.

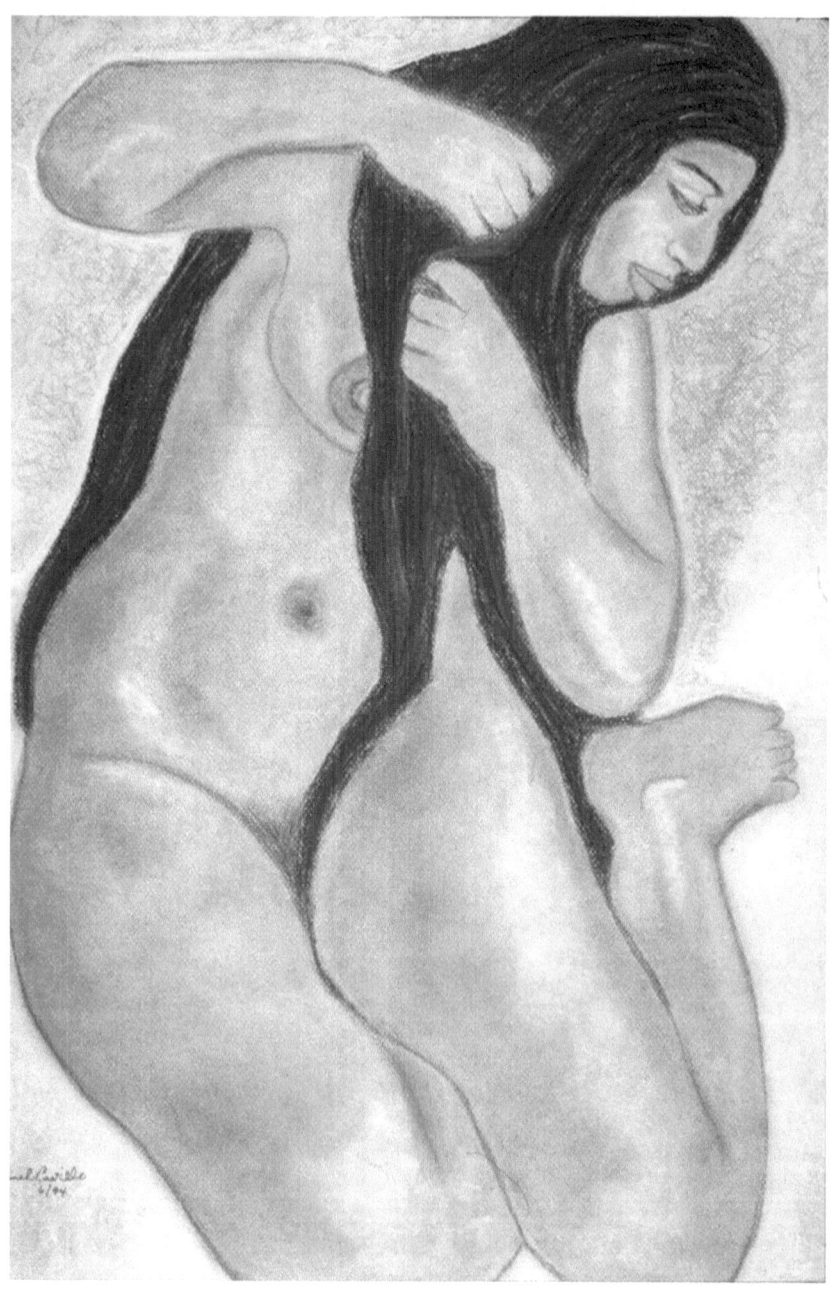

Plate 17. Carmel Castillo, *La India de la Tierra,* 1994, oil pastel on paper, 24" x 30". Reproduced by permission of the artist.

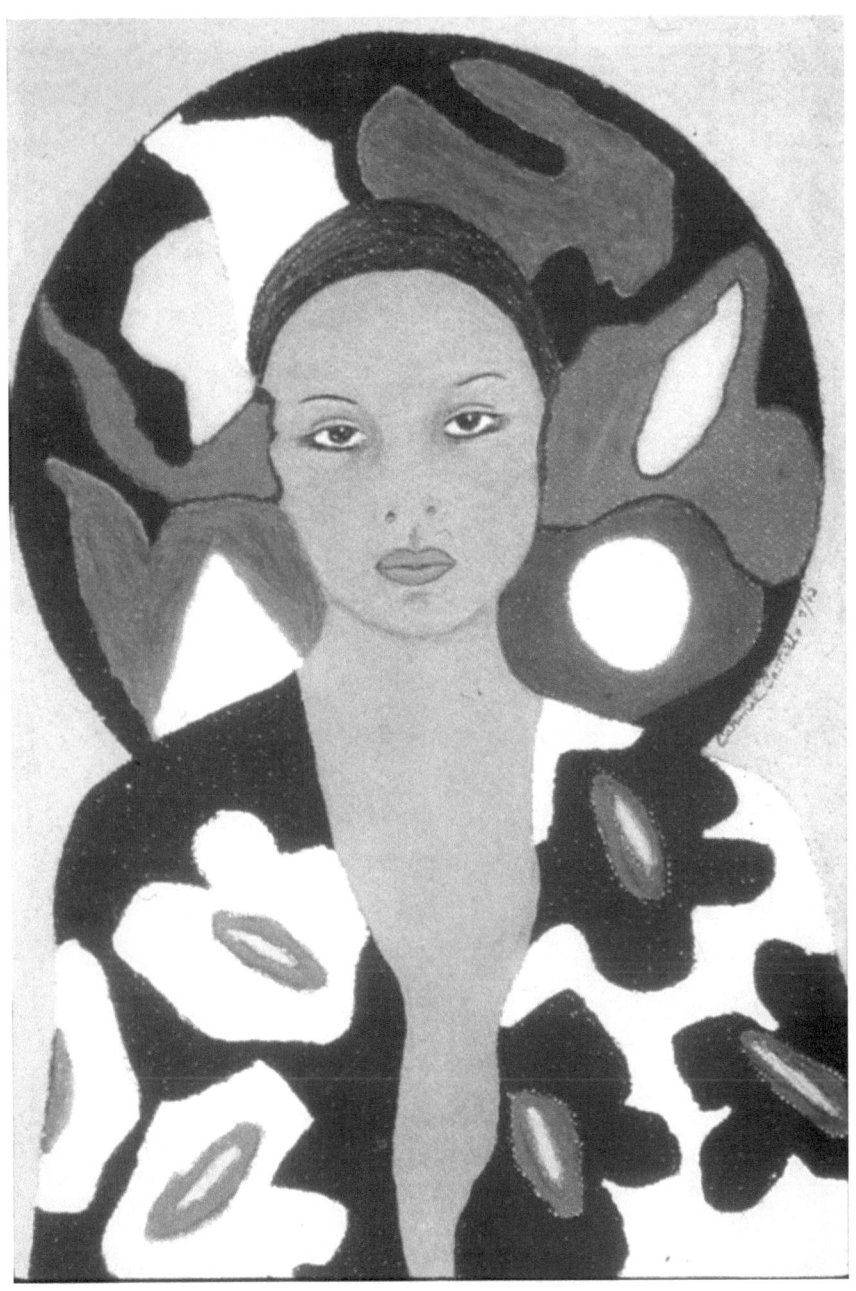

Plate 18. Carmel Castillo, *La Curandera,* 1992, oil pastel on paper, 24″ x 30″.
Reproduced by permission of the artist.

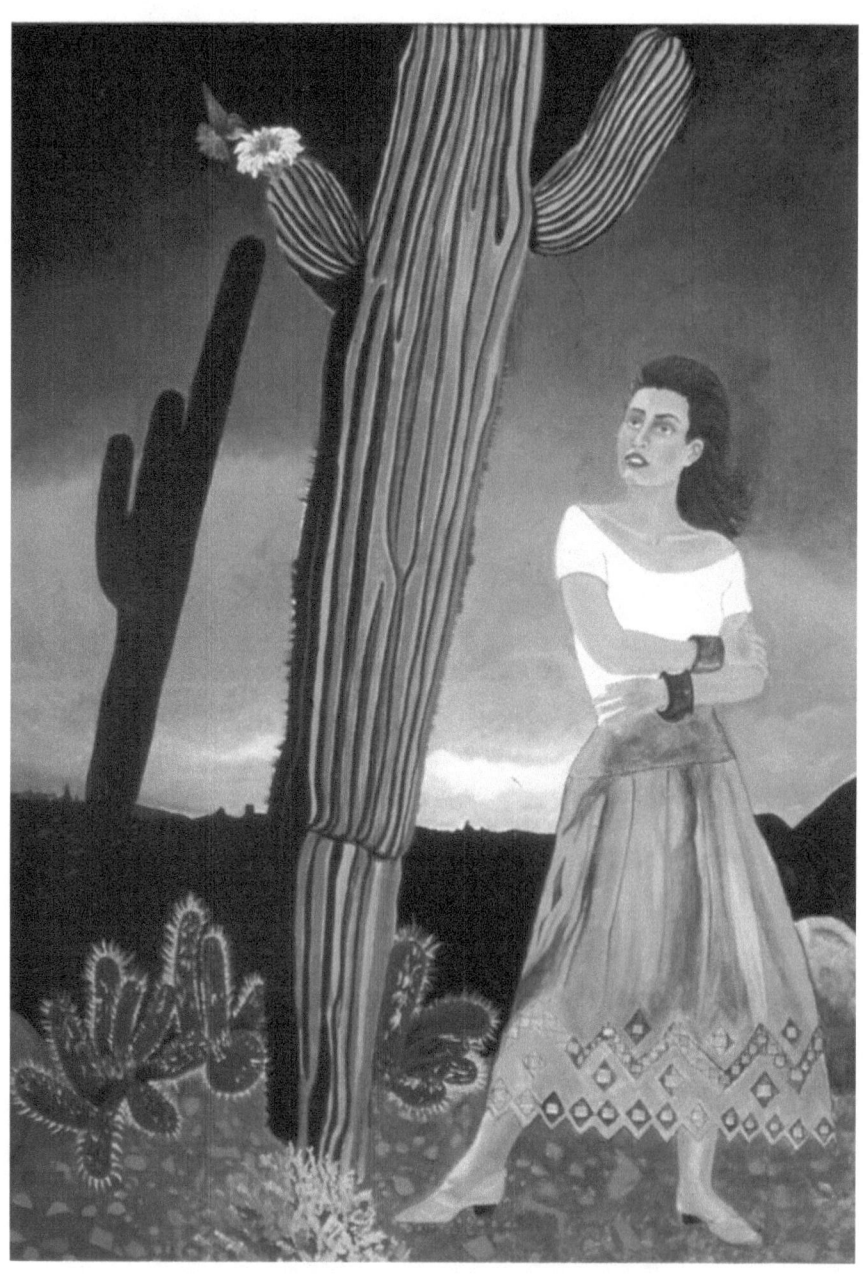

Plate 19. Irma Lerma Barbosa, *Warriors of the New Day,* 1993, oil on canvas, 5' x 4'. Reproduced by permission of the artist.

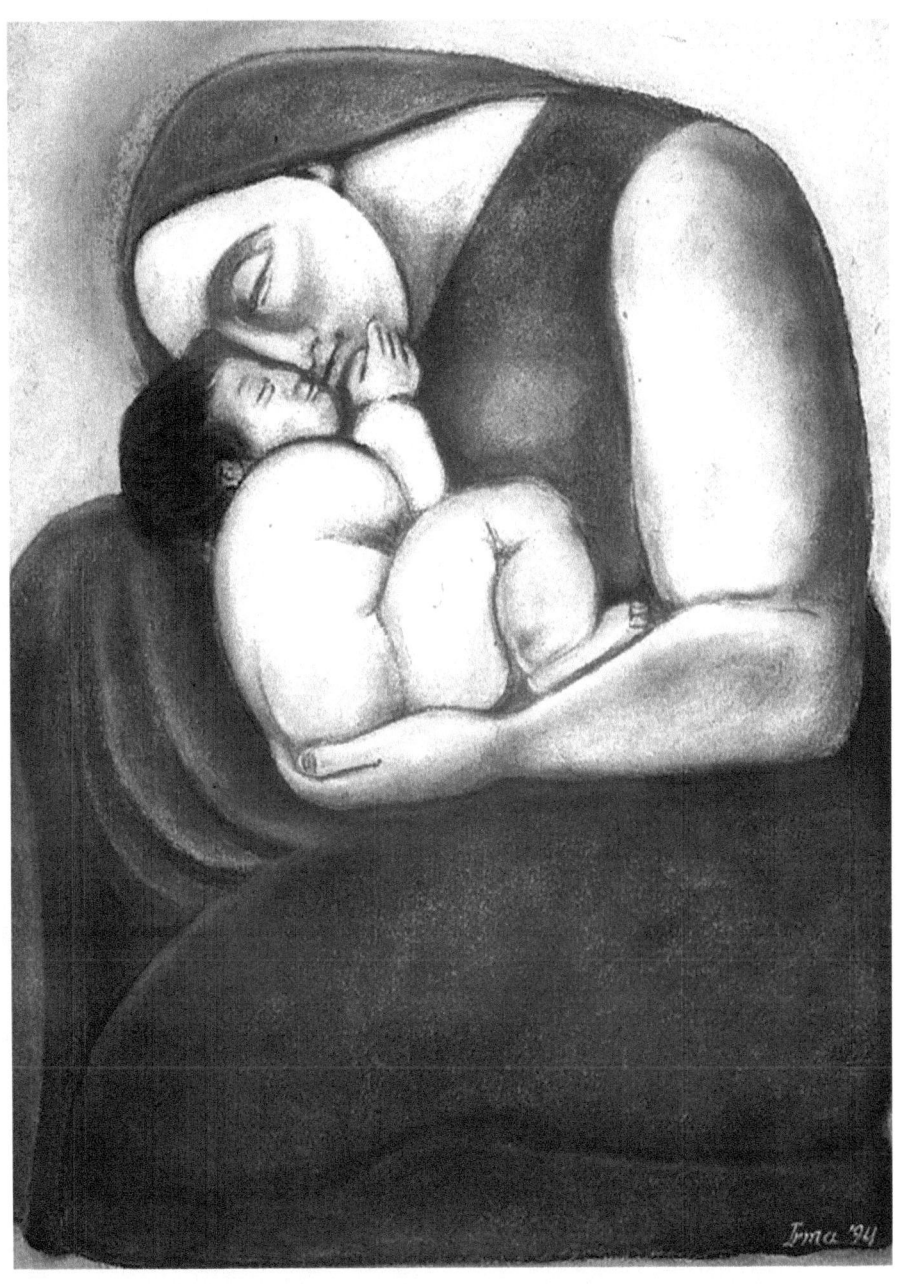

Plate 20. Irma Lerma Barbosa, *Chiapas Madonna,* 1993, oil pastel on paper, 24" x 30". Reproduced by permission of the artist.

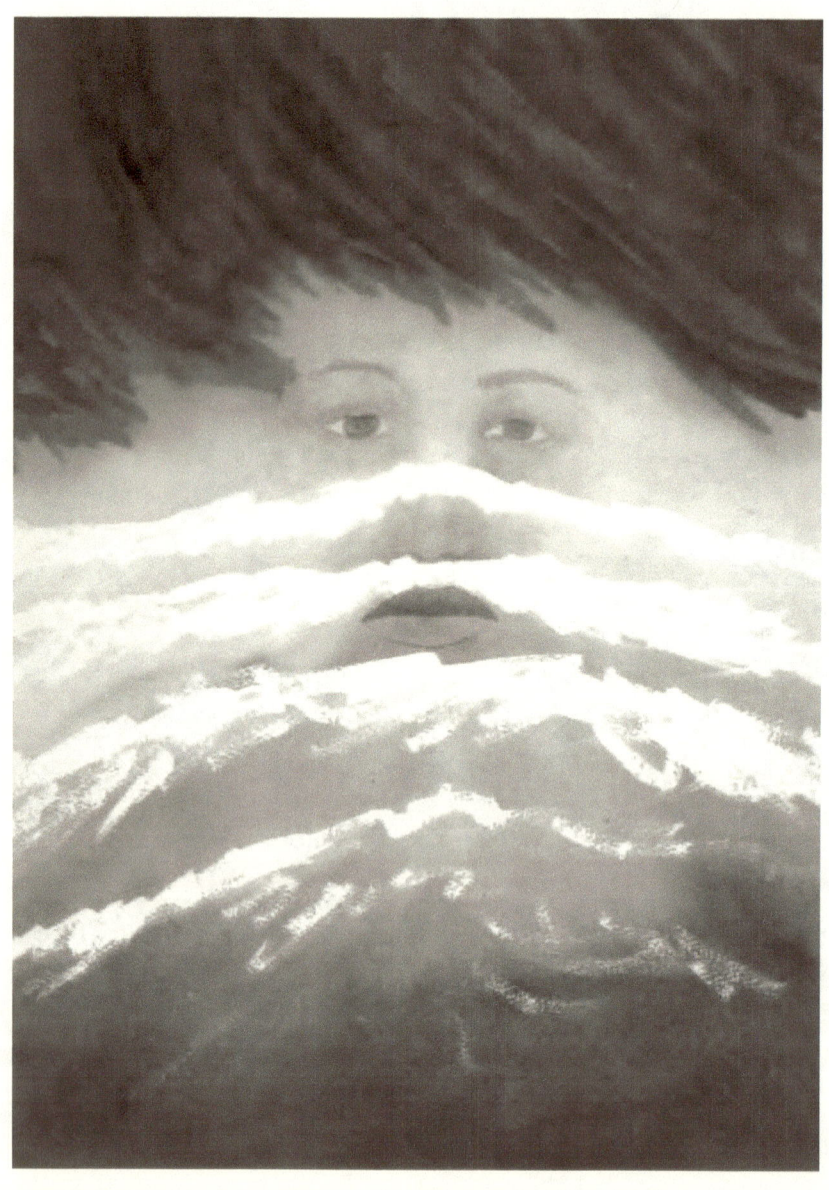

Plate 21 . Laura Llano, *Self-Portrait in Paradise*, 1992, watercolor on paper, 30" x 24". Reproduced by permission of the artist.

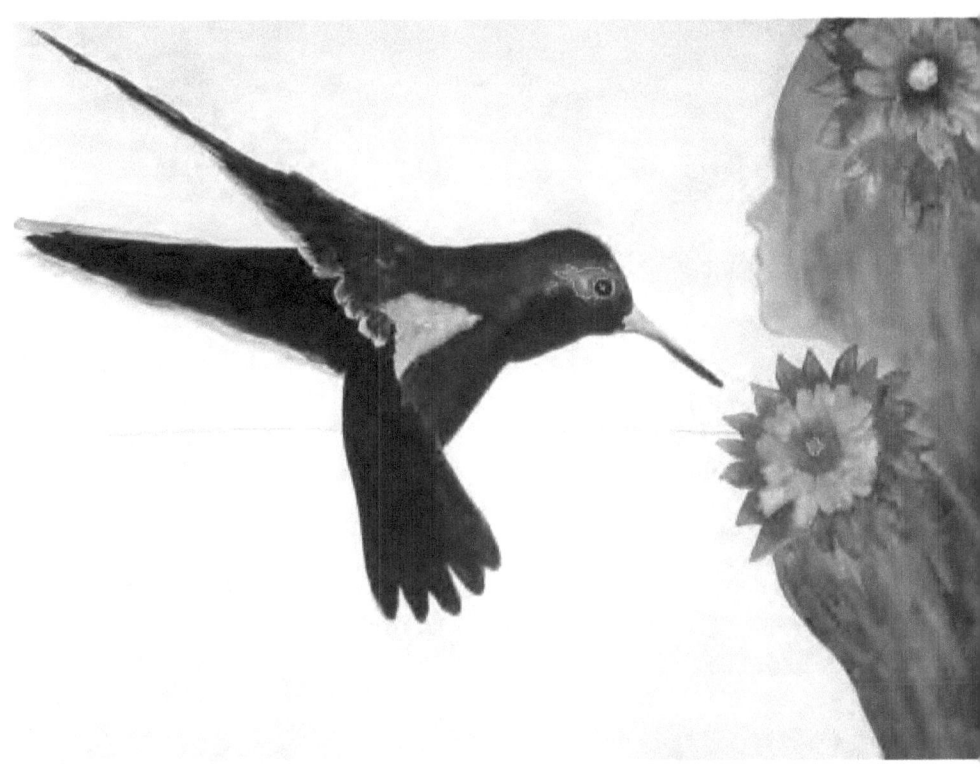

Plate 22. Laura Llano, *The Gift,* 1994, watercolor on paper, 30" x 24". Reproduced by permission of the artist.

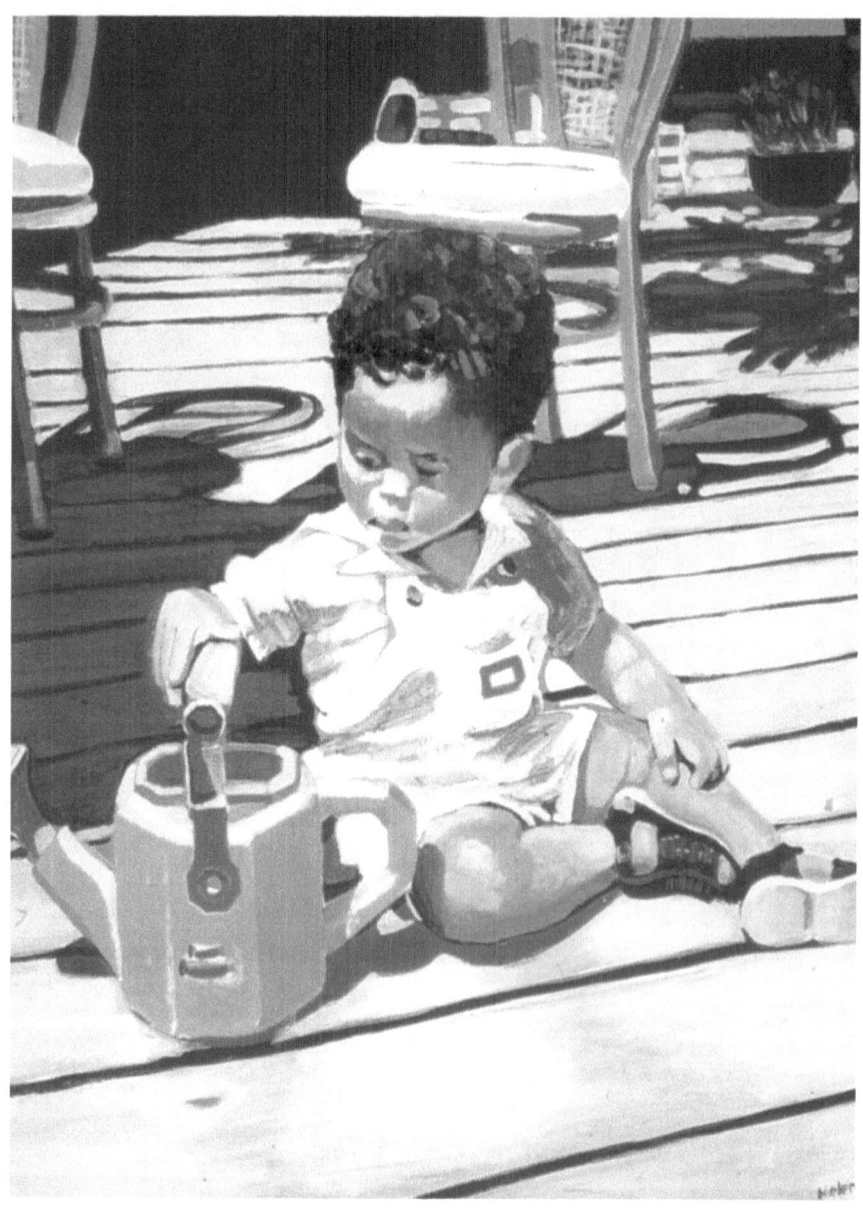

Plate 23. Helen Villa, *Joseph*, 1992, acrylic on canvas, 3′ x 4′. Reproduced by permission of the artist.

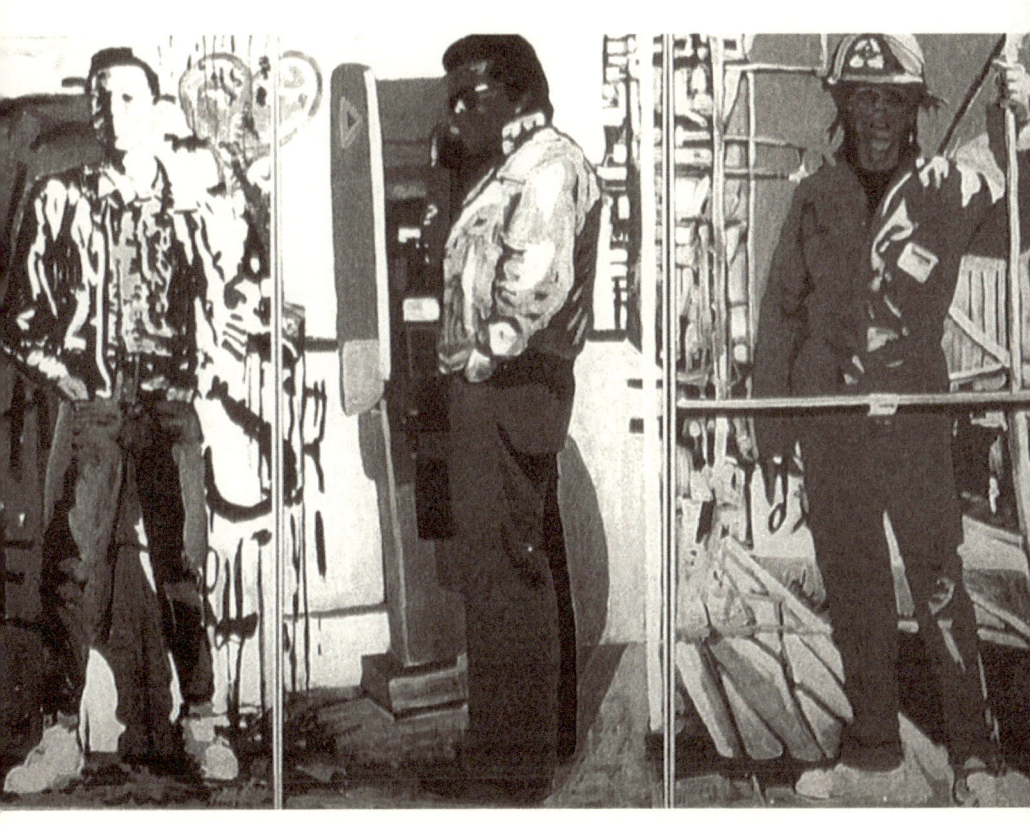

Plate 24. Helen Villa, *Rene, Esteban, and Nathan,* 1993, acrylic on canvas, 4' x 6'. Reproduced by permission of the artist.

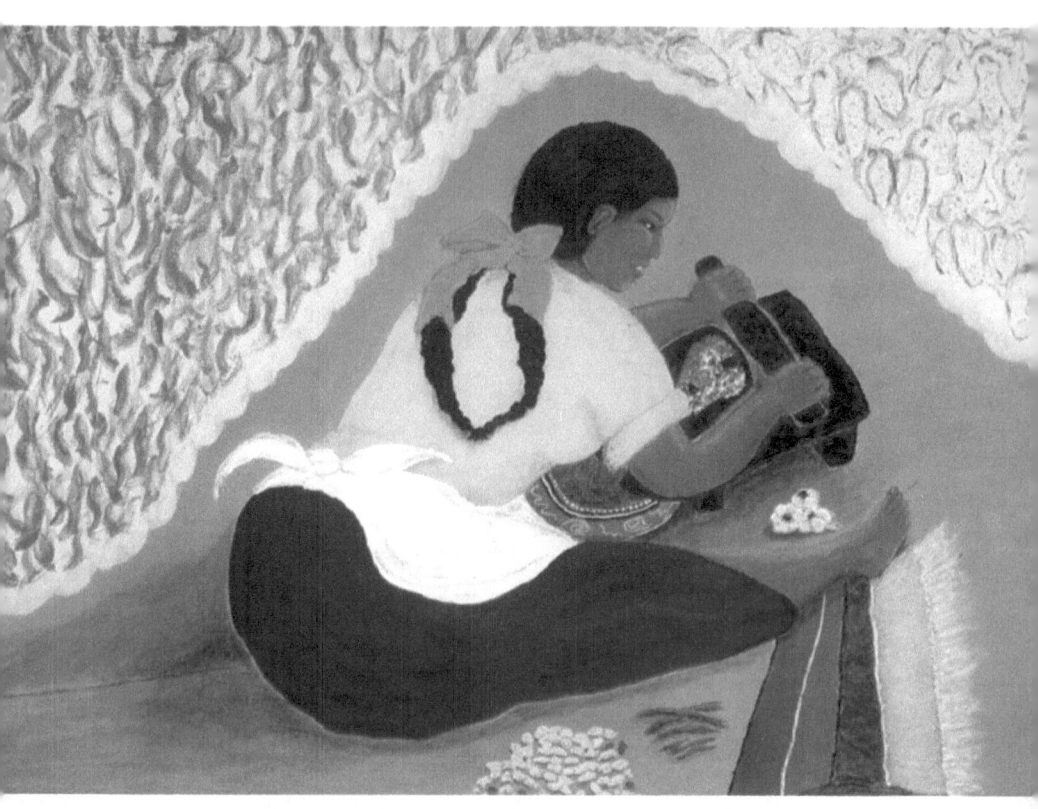

Plate 25. Mareia de Socorro, *The Curtain Rises on Mole,* 1994, acrylic on canvas, 32" x 36". Reproduced by permission of the artist.

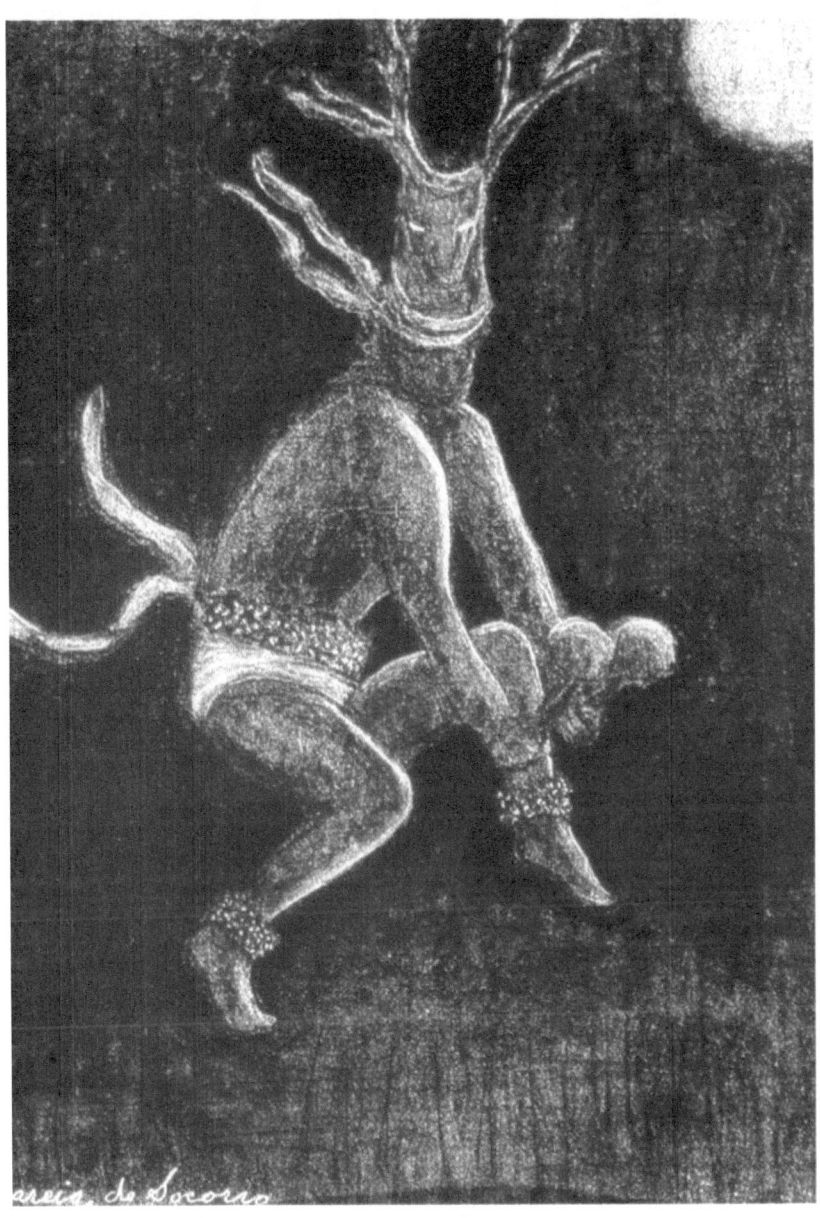

Plate 26. Mareia de Socorro, *The Deer Dances,* 1994, charcoal on paper, 20.5" x 30.5". Reproduced by permission of the artist.

Bibliography

Personal Interviews

Arellano, Lucero. August 23, 1994. Sacramento, California.

Baca, Judith. October 15, 1994, Venice, California.

Barbosa, Irma Lerma. July 25, 1994. Elk Grove, California.

———. August 22, 1994. Sacramento, California.

Castillo, Carmel. June 15, 1994. Citrus Heights, California.

Hernández, Ester. September 17, 1993. San Francisco, California.

Llano, Laura. July 25, 1994. Sacramento, California.

Luna, Chris. June 15, 1994. Sacramento, California.

Méndez, Consuelo. November 13, 1994. Caracas, Venezuela (by telephone).

Montoya Rhodes, Lucy. August 22, 1994. Sacramento, California.

Montoya, Malaquías. October 4, 1994. Elmira, California.

Pérez, Irene. September 20, 1993. Oakland, California.

Rodríguez, Patricia. October 21, 1999. San Francisco, California.

de Socorro, Mareia. June 15, 1994. Sacramento, California.

Villa, Esteban. June 15, 1994. Sacramento, California.

Villa, Helen. June 15, 1994. Sacramento, California.

Secondary Sources

Aaron, Jane, and Sylvia Walby, eds. *Out of the Margins: Women's Studies in the Nineties.* London: Falmer Press, 1991.

Albright, Thomas. "Three Remarkable Latin Murals." *San Francisco Chronicle,* June 7, 1974.

Almaguer, Tomás. *Racial Faultlines: The Historical Origins of White Supremacy in California.* Berkeley: University of California Press, 1994.

Ambiente: Chicano/Latino Arts and Culture in San Francisco. Galería de la Raza, 1990.

Anderson, Benedict. *Imagined Communities: Reflections on the Origin and Spread of Nationalism.* London: Verso, 1983.

Anzaldúa, Gloria. *Borderlands/La Frontera: The New Mestiza.* San Francisco: Spinsters/Aunt Lute, 1989.

————, ed. *Haciendo Caras: Making Face, Making Soul, Creative and Critical Perspectives by Feminists of Color.* San Francisco: Aunt Lute Foundation, 1990.

Art of the Other México: Sources and Meanings. Chicago: Mexican Fine Arts Center Museum, 1993.

Barnett, Alan W. *Community Murals: The People's Art.* Philadelphia: Art Alliance Press, 1984.

Behar, Ruth. *Translated Woman: Crossing the Border with Esperanza's Story.* Boston: Beacon Press, 1993.

Berger, Maurice. *How Art Becomes History: Essays on Art, Society, and Culture in Post–New Deal America.* New York: HarperCollins, 1992.

Blea, Irene I. *La Chicana and the Intersection of Race, Class, and Gender.* New York: Praeger, 1992.

Body/Culture: Chicano Figuration. Sonoma: California State University, Sonoma Gallery, 1990.

Brah, Avtar. "Questions of Difference and International Feminism." In *Out of the Margins: Women's Studies in the Nineties,* ed. Jane Aaron and Sylvia Walby. London: Falmer Press, 1991.

Brown, Betty Ann. "Chicanas Speak Out." *Community Murals Magazine* (spring 1984).

Broyles-González, Yolanda. *El Teatro Campesino: Theater in the Chicano Movement.* Austin: University of Texas Press, 1994.

Bulkin, Elly, Minnie Bruce Pratt, and Barbara Smith. *Yours in Struggle: Three Feminist Perspectives on Anti-Semitism and Racism.* Ithaca, N.Y.: Firebrand Books, 1988.

Burciaga, José Antonio. *Drink Cultura: Chicanismo.* Santa Barbara, Calif.: Joshua Odell Publications, Capra Press, 1993.

CARA: Chicano Art: Resistance and Affirmation, 1965–1985. Los Angeles: Regents of the University of California, 1991.

Carlos Licón: A Retrospective. Sacramento: La Raza/Galería Posada, 1989.

Castillo, Ana. "Feminist Visions." *Crossroads Magazine* 31, May 1993.

————. *Massacre of the Dreamers: Essays on Xicanisma.* Albuquerque: University of New Mexico Press, 1994.

Chabram-Dernersesian, Angie. "Chicana/o Studies as Oppositional Ethnography." *Cultural Studies: Special Issue on Chicana/o Cultural Representations* 4, no. 3 (1990).

Chabram-Dernersesian, Angie, and Rosa Linda Fregoso, eds. *Cultural Studies: Special Issue on Chicana/o Cultural Representation* 4, no. 3 (1990).

Chadwick, Whitney. *Women, Art, and Society.* London: Thames and Hudson, 1980.

Chávez, César E. "El Plan de Delano." *El Malcriado,* March 17, 1966.

The Chicano Codices: Encountering Art of the Americas. San Francisco: The Mexican Museum, 1992.

Clifford, James. *The Predicament of Culture: Twentieth-Century Ethnography, Literature, and Art.* Cambridge, Mass.: Harvard University Press, 1988.

Cockcroft, Eva. "Women in the Community Mural Movement." *Community Murals Magazine* (1976).

Cockcroft, Eva Sperling, and Holly Barnet-Sánchez, eds. *Signs from the Heart: California Chicano Murals.* Albuquerque: University of New Mexico Press, 1990.

Cockcroft, Eva, John Pitman Weber, and James Cockcroft. *Toward a People's Art: The Contemporary Mural Movement.* 2d ed. Albuquerque: University of New Mexico Press, 1998.

Co-Madres Artistas: Story/Visions from the Cactus Tree: A Catalogue of Fine Art. Sacramento: California Arts Council, 1994.

Cotera, Marta. *Diosa y Hembra: The History and Heritage of Chicanas in the U.S.* Austin: Information Systems Development, 1976

————. ."Among the Feminists: Racist, Classist, Issues 1976." *The Chicana Feminist.* Austin: Information Systems Development, 1977.

Counter Colón-Ialismo. San Diego: Centro Cultural de la Raza, 1991.

Covarrubias, Miguel. *Indian Art of Mexico and Central America.* New York: Alfred A. Knopf, 1957.

Daniel, Margaret Rose. "Exhibiting Difference: Aesthetic Politics and Lesbian of Color Film and Video Curatorial Practice." Ph.D. diss., University of California, Santa Cruz, 2001.

Davis, Angela Y. *Women, Race, and Class.* New York: Vintage Books, 1983.

————. *Women, Culture, and Politics.* New York: Vintage Books, 1989.

de la Torre, Adela, and Beatríz Pesquera, eds. *Building with Our Hands: New Directions in Chicana Studies.* Berkeley: University of California Press, 1993.

de Lauretis, Teresa. "Feminist Studies/Critical Studies: Issues, Terms, and Contexts." In *Feminist Studies/Critical Studies,* ed. Teresa de Lauretis. Bloomington: Indiana University Press, 1986.

Día de los Muertos. Chicago: Mexican Fine Arts Center Museum, 1991.

Drescher, Timothy W. *San Francisco Murals: Community Creates Its Muse.* 2d ed. St. Paul, Minn.: Pogo Press, 1994.

Dunitz, Robin J., and James Prigoff. *Painting the Towns: Murals of California.* Los Angeles: RJD Enterprises, 1997.

Dunne, John Gregory. *Delano.* Rev. ed. New York: Noonday Press, 1971.

Ferguson, Russell, Martha Gever, and Trinh T. Minh-ha, eds. *Out There: Marginalization and Contemporary Cultures.* New York: New Museum of Contemporary Art, 1990.

Fernández, Justino. *A Guide to Mexican Art, from Its Beginnings to the Present.* Trans. Joshua C. Taylor. Chicago: University of Chicago Press, 1969.

Flóres, William V., and Rina Benmayor, eds. *Latino Cultural Citizenship: Claiming Identity, Space, and Rights.* Boston: Beacon Press, 1997.

Frankenberg, Ruth. *White Women, Race Matters: The Social Construction of Whiteness.* Minneapolis: University of Minnesota Press, 1993.

García, Alma, ed. *Chicana Feminist Thought: The Basic Historical Writings.* New York: Routledge, 1997.

Garcia, Rupert. "An Historical Look at Raza Murals and Muralists." *El Tecolote* 2, no. 14 (July 1972).

García Canclini, Néstor. *Transforming Modernity: Popular Culture in Mexico.* Trans. Lidia Lozano. Austin: University of Texas Press, 1993.

———. *Hybrid Cultures: Strategies for Entering and Leaving Modernity.* Trans. Christopher L. Chiappari and Silvia L. López. Minneapolis: University of Minnesota Press, 1995.

Gilroy, Paul, Lawrence Grossberg, and Angela McRobbie, eds. *Without Guarantees: In Honour of Stuart Hall.* London: Verso, 2000.

Gluck, Sherna Berger, and Daphne Patai, eds. *Women's Words: The Feminist Practice of Oral History.* London: Routledge, 1991.

Goldman, Shifra M. "Chicano Art: Looking Backward." *Artweek,* June 20, 1981.

———. "Conference Report: Meridian's Art of the Americas: Junctures and Disjunctures." *Community Murals Magazine* (winter 1985).

———. *Dimensions of the Americas: Art and Social Change in Latin America and the United States.* Chicago: University of Chicago Press, 1994.

Goldman, Shifra M., and Tomás Ybarra-Frausto. *Arte Chicano: A Comprehensive Bibliography of Chicano Art, 1965–1981.* Berkeley: Chicano Studies Library Publications Unit, University of California, 1985.

Grossberg, Lawrence, Cary Nelson, and Paula Treichler, eds. *Cultural Studies.* New York: Routledge, 1992.

Hammerback, John C., and Richard J. Jensen. *The Rhetorical Career of César Chavez.* College Station: Texas A&M University Press, 1998.

Hammerback, John C., Richard J. Jensen, and José Ángel Gutiérrez. *A War of Words: Chicano Protest in the 1960s and 1970s.* Westport, Conn.: Greenwood Press, 1985.

Harvey, David. *The Condition of Postmodernity: An Enquiry into the Origins of Cultural Change.* Cambridge: Basil Blackwell, 1989.

hooks, bell. *Feminist Theory: From Margin to Center.* Boston: South End Press, 1984.

Hurtado, Aida. "Relating to Privilege: Seduction and Rejection in the Subordination of White Women and Women of Color." *Signs* 14, no. 4 (1989).

Jay, Martin. *The Dialectical Imagination; A History of the Frankfurt School and the Institute of Social Research, 1923-1950.* Boston: Little, Brown, 1973.

Jiménez, Francisco. "Artistas out in the Cold Again." *ChisméArte* 1, no. 4 (1977).

Karp, Ivan, and Steven D. Lavine, eds. *Exhibiting Cultures: The Poetics and Politics of Museum Display.* Washington, D.C.: Smithsonian Institution Press, 1991.

Kramer, Jane. *Whose Art Is It?* Durham, N.C.: Duke University Press, 1994.

Kranich, Kimberly. "A Bibliography of Periodicals by and about Women of Color." *Feminist Teacher* 5, no. 1 (1990).

LaDuke, Betty. *Women Artists: Multi-Cultural Visions.* Trenton, N.J.: Red Sea Press, 1992.

Lamphere, Louise, Patricia Zavella, Felipe González, with Peter B. Evans. *Sunbelt Working Mothers: Reconciling Family and Factory.* Ithaca: Cornell University Press, 1993.

The Latin American Spirit: Art and Artists in the United States, 1920–1970. New York: The Bronx Museum and Harry N. Abrams, 1988.

Latina Art: Showcase '87. Chicago: Mexican Fine Arts Center Museum, 1987.

Lo del Corazón: Heartbeat of a Culture. San Francisco: Mexican Museum, 1986.

Lorde, Audre. *Sister/Outsider: Essays and Speeches.* Trumansberg, N.Y.: Crossing Press, 1982.

Markham, Roberta H., and Peter T. Markham. *The Flayed God: The Mesoamerican Mythological Tradition: Sacred Texts and Images from Pre-Columbian Mexico and Central America.* San Francisco: Harper–San Francisco, 1992.

Martínez, Elizabeth. "Chingón Politics." *Z Magazine* (April 1990).

———. "Beyond Black/White: The Racisms of Our Time." *Social Justice* 20, nos. 1–2 (spring–summer 1993).

———. "Cinco de Mayo: Latinas with Attitude." *Crossroads* 31 (May 1993).

Matthiessen, Peter. *Sal Si Puedes: César Chávez and the New American Revolution.* New York: Dell, 1969.

Mesa-Bains, Amalia. "A Study of the Influence of Culture on the Development of Identity Among a Group of Chicana Artists." Ph.D. diss., The Wright Institute, 1983.

Mesa-Bains, Amalia, and Ray Patlán. *Social History through Murals: A Teacher's Handbook.* San Francisco: San Francisco Unified School District, 1988.

The Mexican Muralists. Ghent: Museum voor Schone Kunsten, 1993.

Mission Mural Walk Map. San Francisco: Precita Eyes Mural Arts Center, 1993.

Mohanty, Chandra Talpade. "Cartographies of Struggle: Third World Women and the Politics of Feminism." In *Third World Women and the Politics of Feminism.* Ed. Chandra Talpade Mohanty, Ann Russo, and Lourdes Torres. Bloomington: Indiana University Press, 1991.

Mohanty, Chandra Talpade, Ann Russo, and Lourdes Torres, eds. *Third World Women and the Politics of Feminism.* Bloomington: Indiana University Press, 1991.

Montoya, Malaquías, and Leslie Salkowitz-Montoya. "A Critical Perspective on the State of Chicano Art." *Metamorfosis* (1981).

Moraga, Cherríe, and Gloria Anzaldúa, eds. *This Bridge Called My Back: Writings by Radical Women of Color.* New York: Kitchen Table: Women of Color Press, 1983.

Morgan, Robin, ed. *Sisterhood Is Powerful: An Anthology of Writing from the Women's Liberation Movement.* New York: Vintage Press, 1970.

Nieto Gómez, Ana. "Chicanas in the Labor Force." *Encuentro Feminil* 1, no. 2 (1974).

———. "La Feminista." *Encuentro Feminil* 1, no. 2 (1974).

———. "Chicana Feminism." *Caracol* 2, no. 5 (1976).

O'Brien, Mark, and Craig Little, eds. *Reimaging America: The Arts of Social Change.* Philadelphia: New Society Publishers, 1990.

Ochoa, María. "Cooperative Re/Weavings." Mexican American Studies and Research Center, University of Arizona. *Perspectives in Mexican American Studies* 5 (1995).

———. "Feminist Literary Contributions of Gloria Anzaldúa and Cherríe Moraga." Paper presented at the First International MELUS Conference, Honolulu, HI, April 1997.

Paz, Octavio. *Essays on Mexican Art.* Trans. Helen Lane. New York: Harcourt Brace & Co., 1993.

Quintana, Alvina E. *Home Girls: Chicana Literary Voices.* Philadelphia: Temple University Press, 1996.

Quintero, Victoria. "A Mural Is a Painting on a Wall Done by Human Hands." *El Tecolote* 5, no. 1 (1974).

Quirarte, Jacinto. *Mexican American Artists.* Austin: University of Texas Press, 1973

———..*Chicano Art History: A Book of Selected Readings.* Austin: University of Texas Press, 1984.

Raven, Arlene, Cassandra Langer, and Joanna Frueh, eds. *Feminist Art Criticism: An Anthology.* New York: HarperCollins, 1991.

Rodríguez, Patricia. *Selected Readings on Chicano Art.* Berkeley: Chicano Studies Program, University of California, 1977.

Rosaldo, Renato. *Culture and Truth: The Remaking of Social Analysis.* Boston: Beacon Press, 1989.

Roth, Moira, ed. *Connecting Conversations: Interviews with 28 Bay Area Women Artists.* Oakland, Calif.: Eucalyptus Press, 1988.

Ruiz, Vicki and Carol DuBois, eds. *Unequal Sisters: A Multicultural Reader in U.S. Women's History.* London: Routledge, 1990.

Salazar, Ruben. "Who Is a Chicano? And What Is It the Chicanos Want?" *Los Angeles Times,* February 6, 1970.

Sandoval, Chela. "U.S. Third World Feminism: The Theory and Method of Oppositional Consciousness in the Postmodern World." *Genders* 10 (spring 1991).

———. *Methodology of the Oppressed.* Theory Out of Bounds series. Minneapolis: University of Minnesota Press, 2000.

Tsing, Anna Lowenhaupt. *In the Realm of the Diamond Queen: Marginality in an Out of the Way Place.* Princeton: Princeton University Press, 1993.

Váldez, Luis, and Stan Steiner, eds. *Aztlán: An Anthology of Mexican American Literature.* New York: Alfred A. Knopf, 1972.

Vásquez, Enriqueta Longeaux. "¡Despierten Hermanas! The Women of La Raza Part II." *El Grito del Norte* 2, no. 10 (1969).

Venegas, Sybil. "The Artists and Their Work: The Social Role of the Chicana Artist." *ChisméArte* 1, no. 4 (1977).

———. "Conditions for Producing Chicana Art." *ChisméArte* 1, no. 4 (1977).

Wilds, Deborah J. "Students of Color Make Gains in Higher Education." *American Council on Education Office of Minorities in Higher Education, 17th Annual Status Report* 49, no. 3 (2000).

Williams, Raymond. *Problems in Materialism and Culture: Selected Essays.* London: Verso, 1980.

———. *Resources of Hope: Culture, Democracy, Socialism.* London: Verso, 1989.

Wolff, Janet. *The Social Production of Art.* London: Cambridge University Press, 1983.

———. *Feminine Sentences: Essays on Women and Culture.* Berkeley: University of California Press, 1990.

———. *Aesthetics and the Sociology of Art.* 2d ed. Ann Arbor: University of Michigan Press, 1993.

Yau, John. "Please Wait by the Cloakroom." In *Out There: Marginalization and Contemporary Cultures.* Ed. Russell Ferguson, Martha Gever, and Trinh T. Minh-ha. New York: Museum of Contemporary Art, 1990.

Ybarra-Frausto, Tomás. "Recuerdo, Descubrimiento, Voluntad: Mexican/Chicano Customs for Day of the Dead." In *Día de los Muertos*. Chicago: Mexican Fine Arts Center Museum, 1991.

Zavella, Patricia. "Feminist Insider Dilemmas: Constructing Identity with 'Chicana' Informants." *Frontiers: A Journal of Women's Studies* 13, no. 3 (1992).

———. Women's Work and Chicano Families: Cannery Workers of the Santa Clara Valley. Ithaca: Cornell University Press, 1987.

Index

Adelita, 71
Alicia, Juana, xvii, 38, 57n. 14
altar-installations, 37, 56n. 12, 82
Anderson, Benedict, 22
Anzaldúa, Gloria, 20, 28
art: as form of critical reflection, 28; and
  political activism, 28; as therapy, 73
artistic chauvinism, 24
artists: as cultural workers, 5; relationship
  with public, 46, 88. See also Chicano/a
  artists; creative collectives
Art/Women/California, 1950–2000:
  Parallels and Intersections (exhibition),
  xvi
Aztec deities, mythos of, 20, 52, 71,
  89–90
Aztec Earth Monster, 52
Aztec migration myth, 71

Balmy Alley murals, 33, 38, 39, **94, 95**
Barbosa, Irma Lerma, 27, 59, 60, 61, 64,
  68–72, 82, 84n. 1, 91; works by, **116,
  117**
Barnett, Alan, 46, 47
Behar, Ruth, 4, 6, 11
Benmayor, Rina, 4, 6, 7
Bergman, Miranda, 38, 57n. 14
Blea, Irene, 84n. 5
blessing of the four directions, 82, 83
Boone, Edythe, 57n. 14

Brah, Avtar, 4
Broyles-González, Yolanda, 5, 24

Café Luna, 3
California Arts Council, 62; grant from,
  81
Carrillo, Graciela, xvii, 33, 36, 38, 39, 40,
  41, 54, 55, 91; works by, **95**
Castillo, Ana, 27
Castillo, Carmel, 59, 61, 64, 65–68, 81,
  82, 84n. 1, 91; works by, **114, 115**
Cervantes, Susan Kelk, 38, 55, 57n. 14,
  57n. 23
Chabram-Dernersesian, Angie, 4
Chávez, César E., 18, 25; postage stamp
  commemorating, 57n. 20
Chiapas Madonna (painting), 68, 71, **117**
Chicana artistry: and Chicano art
  community, xvi
Chicana feminism, 19, 43–44
Chicana/o artists: and self-determination,
  5; unsigned work of, 24
Chicana/o Art Movement, 1–9, 24, 53,
  55–56, 71, 83, 88; and sexual politics,
  27
Chicanas: and feminist critiques, 18; and
  higher education, 13; neglect of
  aesthetic contributions by, xv–xvii, 90;
  as subordinated agents, 25
Chicano cultural nationalism, 18

Chicano Movement, 16, 17; subordinate positions for women in, 18
C. N. Gorman Museum, 65
Coatlicue: statue of, xv–xvi, 89–90; as threat to Roman Catholic church, xvi
Co-Madres Artistas, 1–12, 21, 25, 26, 29, 59–91; acquiring exhibition space, 88; birth of, 60; and blessing of the four directions, 82, 83; funding of, 62, 81, 88; identification as Chicanas, 22; interviewing members of, 8–9, 11–12; modes of production and individual creativity, 16; past tensions within, 81; roles as comadres, 83; as social agents and cultural workers, 63; stability of, 89; use of varied media, 59; volunteer work by, 4; works by, **114–24**
Co-Madre Enchiladas: . . . Diez Años (exhibition), 83
community, 7, 26; art-related projects benefiting, 40; belonging to, 80–84; doing artwork for, 39; with flexible cultural boundaries, 88; imagined, 22; and interactions with artists, 34; presentation of *Latinoamerica* to, 53; service to, 77
la conciencia mestiza, 20
Cotera, Marta, 19
creative collectives, 1, 5, 15, 90
cultural citizenship, 7
cultural practices: alternative and oppositional, 16
The Curtain Rises on Mole (painting), 79, 122

Davis, Angela Y., 28
The Deer Dances (painting), 80, **123**
Desai, Meera, 57n. 14
devil dancers, 51, 52
Dia de los Muertos, 73
differential oppositional consciousness, 36–37
Diosa y Hembra: The History and Heritage of Chicanas in the United States (Cotera), 19
Drescher, Timothy W., 4, 45

El Teatro Campesino, 24–25
Encuentro Feminil, 13n. 1, 19
ethnographic authority, 6
ethnography, 4, 11
Evans, Peter B., 6

exhibitions, 60, 80; *Art/Women/California, 1950-2000: Parallels and Intersections*, xvi; *Co-Madre Enchiladas: . . . Diez Años*, 83; *First Front: Vanguard of the Chicano Movement in Northern California*, xvi; *Historias de Esperanza/Stories of Hope*, 82; use of ritual blessings to open, 82

Fantasy World for Children (mural), 33, 40, 55, **112, 113**
fecundity and regeneration, 52
Fernández, Justino, 89–90
First Front: Vanguard of the Chicano Movement in Northern California (exhibition), xvi
Francher, Brooke, 38
Frankenberg, Ruth, 6, 12
La Frontera, 20

La Galería de la Raza, xvi, 2, 3, 23, 24, 44, 55, 90
García Canclini, Néstor, 87–88
García, Eva, xvii
García, Lorraine, xvii, 84n. 6
García, Rupert, 44
Garcia Smith, Katherine, 84n. 1
gender, 5, 11, 17, 27
The Gift (painting), 74, **119**
Gluck, Sherna Berger, 6
Goldman, Shifra, 4, 25, 27
Gómez, Ana Nieto, 3, 19
Gonzales, Felipe, 6

Harlan, Theresa, 26, 65, 83–84
heritage murals, 47
Hernández, Carol, 84n. 6
Hernández, Ester, xvi, xvii, 27, 34, 35, 40, 41, 42, 43, 44, 45, 46, 54, 57n. 23, 91; painting a panel, **110**
Historias de Esperanza/Stories of Hope (exhibition), 82
Hope: Children of the World (painting), 79
Huerta, Dolores, 18
Huitzilopochtli, 71
hybridity, 87–88

images: cultural vs. political, 55
interviews, 33, 37, 59

Joseph (painting), 76–77, **120**

Kahlo, Frida, 67, 73

La Curandera (painting), 67, **115**
La India de la Tierra (painting), 66–67, **114**
La India Mas Hermosa (painting), 67
LaMarr, Jean, xvi
Lamphere, Louise, 6
Latinas/os, 22; heterogeneity of
    experience, 40
Latinoamerica (mural), 10, 33, 35, 40, 45,
    48–53, 55, **96, 97, 98–99, 100–101**;
    coordinating muralists for, 41;
    dedication of, 53; description of,
    48–50; and multiethnic consciousness,
    47; Navajo symbols in, 49; themes and
    motifs in, 50
lesbians, 2, 50
Licón, Carlos, 61, 66, 67
Littleton, Yvonne, 57n. 14
Llano, Laura, 59, 60, 61, 64, 72–74, 83,
    84n. 1, 91; works by, **118, 119**
Loarca, Carlos, 38
Lomas Garza, Carmen, xvii
López, Yolanda, xvi, xvii, 24, 31n. 49
Lorde, Audre, 37
Los Tres Grandes, 23
Lucero, Linda, xvii

Maestrapeace (mural), 45, 57n. 14
Magonista, 71
maguey and maize, 52
Malintzin, 71
mandalas, 64
Maradiaga, Ralph, 23, 44
Markham, Peter, 70
Markham, Roberta, 70
Méndez, Consuelo, xvii, 33, 34, 35, 36,
    40, 41, 54, 91
mentors, 27
Mesa-Bains, Amalia, xi–xii, xvii, 4, 43–44,
    47, 56n. 12
mestizaje culture, 17, 20, 50, 51
mestiza/o identity and consciousness, 17

methodology of the oppressed, 20
Mexican American identity: ideological
    face of, 5
Mexican American Liberation Art Front,
    85n. 29
misogyny, 18, 19
Mohanty, Chandra Talpade, 5, 21, 22
Montoya, José, 85n. 29
Montoya, Malaquías, 24, 27, 40, 44
Montoya Rhodes, Lucy, 59, 61, 81
Moraga, Cherríe, 20
Mother Earth, 65, 67, 82; imagery of, 66;
    as Madonna, 72
El Movimiento, xvi
Mujeres Muralistas, xvi, 1–12, 21, 25, 26,
    29, 33–56, 87–91; core group, 36;
    eclectic style of, 48; and everyday
    representations, 46; and funding, 41;
    hybridized style of painting, 40;
    identification as Chicanas, 22; internal
    organization of, 36; interviewing
    members of, 8–9, 11–12; lack of
    common style, 40; manifesto of, 35;
    mistaken for men, 44; modes of
    production and individual creativity, 16;
    naming of, 23; no designated leader,
    42; relationship with public, 46; varied
    life experiences and backgrounds of
    artists, 40; volunteer work by, 4; works
    by, **96, 97, 98–99, 100 101, 102, 103,
    104–105, 106–107, 108, 112, 113**
muralists: as catalysts for social change, 46
mural painting: public nature of, 46; work
    requirements of, 34
murals: everyday occurrences as subject
    matter of, 39; *Fantasy World for
    Children*, 33, 40, 55, **112, 113**;
    heritage, 47; high output in San
    Francisco, 38; *Latinoamerica*, 10, 33,
    35, 40, 45, 47, 48–53, 55, **96, 97,
    98–99, 100–101**; longevity of, 34;
    painting over of, 58n. 57; *Para el
    Mercado*, xvi, 10, 33, 40, 47, 53, **102,
    103, 104–105, 106–107**; physical
    demands of creating, 43; and
    reconciliation of cultures, 88;
    Rhomboidal Parallelogram, 33, 40, 54,
    108, 109, 110, 111

Neuman, Osha, 38
Nevel-Guerrero, Xochitl, xvii, 38
Nieto Gómez, Ana, 13n. 1, 19

la ofrenda, 37
Olivo, Miriam, 57n. 23
oppositional consciousness, 20
oral history, 4, 12; and collection
   process, 6

Packard, Emmy Lou, 41
Para el Mercado (mural), xvi, 10, 33, 40,
   102, 103, 104–105, 106–107;
   commissioned by owner of Paco's
   Tacos, 53; dedication of, 54; and Pan-
   American aesthetic, 47
Pasto, Tarmo, 27, 69, 70
Patai, Daphne, 6
Patlán, Ray, 38
Pérez, Irene, xvi, xvii, 27, 33, 34, 35, 36,
   38, 39, 41, 43, 44, 45, 54, 55, 57n. 14;
   emphasis on positive aspects of her
   culture, 42; works by, **94**
Posada, José Guadalupe, 23
practice anthropology, 6
Precita Eyes Mural Arts Center, 54

Quintana, Alvina, 24
Quirarte, Jacinto, 4
quotidian, 1, 7, 87

racism, 20
La Raza Galería Posada, 3, 60, 61, 83
Rene, Esteban, and Nathan (painting), 77,
   121
Rhomboidal Parallelogram (mural), 33, 40,
   54, **108, 111**; framing device for, **109**;
   Hernández at work on, **110**
Rios, Michael, 44–45
Rivera, Diego, 38, 41
Rodríguez, Celia, xvii, 84n. 6
Rodríguez, Patricia, xvi, xvii, 27, 33, 34,
   35, 38, 39, 41, 42, 46, 47, 54, 55, 91,
   91n. 1, **95**; as public spokesperson, 36
Rodríguez, Ruth, 57n. 23
Roman Catholic church, xvi
Rosaldo, Renato, 6, 9
Royal Chicano Air Force, 3, 60, 64, 68, 69,
   75, 84n. 6; flying chiles logo, 77; origin
   of name, 85n. 29

Sacramento State University, 3
Sandoval, Chela, 20, 36
San Francisco Art Institute, 2, 40
San José Museum of Art, xvi, 90
Self-Portrait in Paradise (painting), 74, **118**
Sephardic Jews, 5, 17
sexism, 20
El Sindicato de Pintores y Escultores, 35
Siqueros, David Alfaro, 35
slaves, 17
de Socorro, Mareia, 59, 62, 64, 78–80,
   82–83, 84, 84n. 1, 85n. 19, 91; use of
   a variety of media and techniques, 78;
   works by, **122, 123**
*Story/Visions from the Cactus Tree: A
   Catalogue of Fine Art*, 63

Talamantez, Josie, 82
*This Bridge Called My Back: Writings by
   Radical Women of Color (Anzaldúa and
   Moraga)*, 20, 21
Tlaltecuhtli, 53; Aztec mask of, 52
*Toward a People's Art: The Contemporary
   Mural Movement*, xvi
Tsing, Anna Lowenhaupt, 21

United Farm Workers Union, 4, 10, 25, 28,
   40
University of California, Berkeley, 2, 40
University of California, Davis, 65
U.S. Third World feminism, 2, 5, 12, 16

Vásquez, Enriqueta Longeaux, 18
Venegas, Sybil, 25, 27, 28–29, 40
Villa, Esteban, 64–65, 75, 77, 85n. 29
Villa, Helen, 59, 60, 75–78, 84n. 1, 91; of
   European descent, 75; use of family
   members as subjects, 76; works by,
   120, 121
Virgen de Guadalupe, 25

Warriors of the New Day (painting), 68,
   70, **116**
Williams, Raymond, 16
women: expansion of role of, 18; Puerto
   Rican, 7; roles and tradition, 19; in
   subordinate positions in Chicano
   Movement, 18; traditional role in family,
   17

women of color, 5, 11, 21; alliances
    among, 20–23; treatment of, 90

Yañez, Rene, 44
Ybarra-Frausto, Tomás, 4, 25, 27, 38

Zavella, Patricia, 4, 6
zia, 49, 50, 51
Zuñiga, Francisco, 71